D0730926

4-
2008

What readers are saying about
Core Animation for Mac OS X and the iPhone

Animation isn't "eye candy." It's about making GUI experiences less arbitrary and more comprehensible. The developers of Apple's Core Animation get this, and so does Bill Dudney. His book offers a deep, thoughtful guide to the API and the ideas behind it.

▶ **Chris Adamson**
  Author of *QuickTime for Java: A Developer's Notebook*

It's great to see a book for Mac developers that focuses on one topic and does it well. Its pace is excellent and will allow you to have simple animations running in minutes. As the book goes deeper into its subject, it presents you with just the right amount of information to understand what you are doing so you don't feel like you are just following instructions, yet it never turns into a dry reference manual that overloads you with unnecessary detail.

▶ **Steve ("Scotty") Scott**
  The Mac Developer Network (http://www.macdevnet.com)

Finally! The comprehensive how-to guide we've been waiting for on all our Core Animation needs.

▶ **Eric Wing**
  Developer

As an early adopter of Core Animation technology for the creation of Videator, I have but one regret: if only I had had Bill's book, I would have finished it in half the time!

▶ **Andrew Stone**
  CEO, stone.com

Core Animation is an exciting new library for developers on both the iPhone and the Mac. Bill Dudney's book makes a great companion for Cocoa programmers looking to add it to their bag of developer tricks.

▶ **Daniel Jalkut**
Founder, Red Sweater Software

Apple has abstracted the power of the underlying graphics engine that has been in Mac OS X into a framework we can all use to improve the user experience. Bill Dudney has given us a road map to that framework just as Apple is providing the next new platform: the iPhone SDK. Now it's time for us to make beautiful code.

▶ **Bill Shirley**
Senior Software Architect, Frazer, Ltd.

Core Animation for Mac OS X and the iPhone is that all-too-rare kind of how-to engineering book that is both deeply informative and enjoyable to read. If you want your app to remain competitive in the Mac marketplace, a mastery of Core Animation is crucial. This book will go a long way to getting your UI development skills where they need to be in order to take advantage of the most excited trends in Mac OS on the desktop, the iPhone, and beyond.

▶ **John C. Fox**
Creator of MemoryMiner

The focus on the principles of animation and smooth learning curve makes *Core Animation for Mac OS X and the iPhone* a perfect companion in your transition to the new framework.

▶ **Danny Greg**
Developer, Realmac Software

This book is a great companion to Apple's programming guide. Using this book I was able to easily add user interface animations to my Cocoa application in just a few nights.

▶ **Bill Nalen**
Cocoa Developer

Core Animation for Mac OS X and the iPhone

Creating Compelling Dynamic User Interfaces

Core Animation for Mac OS X and the iPhone
Creating Compelling Dynamic User Interfaces

Bill Dudney

The Pragmatic Bookshelf
Raleigh, North Carolina   Dallas, Texas

Many of the designations used by manufacturers and sellers to distinguish their products are claimed as trademarks. Where those designations appear in this book, and The Pragmatic Programmers, LLC was aware of a trademark claim, the designations have been printed in initial capital letters or in all capitals. The Pragmatic Starter Kit, The Pragmatic Programmer, Pragmatic Programming, Pragmatic Bookshelf and the linking *g* device are trademarks of The Pragmatic Programmers, LLC.

Every precaution was taken in the preparation of this book. However, the publisher assumes no responsibility for errors or omissions, or for damages that may result from the use of information (including program listings) contained herein.

Our Pragmatic courses, workshops, and other products can help you and your team create better software and have more fun. For more information, as well as the latest Pragmatic titles, please visit us at

> http://www.pragprog.com

Copyright © 2008 Bill Dudney.

All rights reserved.

No part of this publication may be reproduced, stored in a retrieval system, or transmitted, in any form, or by any means, electronic, mechanical, photocopying, recording, or otherwise, without the prior consent of the publisher.

Printed in the United States of America.

ISBN-10: 1-934356-10-7

ISBN-13: 978-1-934356-10-4

Printed on acid-free paper.

P1.0 printing, October 2008

Version: 2008-10-2

Contents

To invent, you need a good imagination and a pile of junk.
▶ Thomas A. Edison

Chapter 1

Introduction

Animation has been an important part of the Mac OS X user interface since the beginning. You've probably seen the Genie effect so many times that you hardly notice it anymore. But I still remember the first time I saw a QuickTime movie being minimized via Genie. The movie kept playing as the window shrank and distorted onto the Dock. That knocked my socks off. Or how about the first time you saw the Magnification effect on the Dock? It's not just eye candy, but it *is* beautiful! Even back before there was Mac OS X, there was NeXTstep with its animating Recycle Bin; as the disposed files were deleted, the recycle symbol would animate. That was not nearly as beautiful as what we get today from Mac OS X, but for its time, it was amazing. I would create files just so I could delete them! As the hardware we run on becomes more and more capable, these types of effects become even more natural to add to our applications.

Consider how Apple integrates animation into its operating systems and applications. For example, when users start Front Row, the whole desktop changes to an animation-centric three-dimensional look and feel with smooth animations and beautiful reflections. You'll find animation even when you are working on something as simple as preparing a presentation in Keynote. When a slide in Keynote is moved to another spot in a presentation, the rest of the slides move around to get out of the moving slide's way. Not only does this look great, but it also helps the user understand what their actions are doing. Subtly or dramatically, Keynote and Front Row are keeping their users informed with their use of animation.

Many other applications in Mac OS X and on the iPhone—products both from Apple and from third-party developers—have adopted animation in their user interfaces to make them look better and to improve the overall user experience. Animation is becoming commonplace, so users are starting to expect it. The good news is that implementing animations with Core Animation is easy.

1.1 What Is Core Animation?

Core Animation is a group of features and functionality that makes it easy to build animated user interfaces. Used in its simplest form, Core Animation implicitly animates the properties of views and windows without you having to write any code related to animation. Just tell the view or window that you want animation and change a property, and Core Animation takes care of the rest of the details and smoothly animates the change from the old value to the new value.

Although animation has been possible in Mac OS X since the beginning, it has always taken a lot of time and effort to get things just right. It's not just the aesthetic of the animation that is difficult to get right. Often, the technical complexity of making animated UIs has forced developers to limit their use of animation. Core Animation is not going to relieve us of the aesthetic difficulty of making a beautiful user interface, but it does a great job of relieving us of the technical tedium. Gone are the days of coding threads for animation; now we can fire an animation and forget about it. Core Animation will take care of the details.

You need to think about two things when building animations: the time to completion and the frames that will be needed to smoothly get there. Core Animation takes care of both of these factors and works under the assumption that the end time is more important than getting a certain number of frames in front of the user. Practically what this means is that Core Animation will drop intermediate frames in order to complete the animation on time rather than finish late and show all the frames. Basically, this means as programmers we can't assume that we know exactly how Core Animation will perform an animation up front. Factors such as system load and graphics card capabilities will determine exactly how the animation will appear at runtime.

At its heart, Core Animation is based on a concept called a *layer*, which is a two-dimensional surface that can be animated in three dimensions. Being two-dimensional, layers do not have depth; however, because they can be placed and animated in a 3D space, they can be positioned at different depths, can be rotated, or can be otherwise placed in a scene. This is the trick to the look of applications such as Front

Row or UI elements such as Cover Flow in iTunes or the Finder. The icons that move around on the Lazy Susan–like platter in Front Row as you change a selection in the menu are two-dimensional images placed on a 3D platter and then moved along the outer rim of that platter as you change a selection. Cover art in iTunes is arranged with a perspective transformation so that the unselected album art looks like it was placed behind the selected cover art and rotated slightly. These treatments (and many more) are simple transformations when using Core Animation.

1.2 In This Book

Core Animation became part of Mac OS X in Leopard (10.5) and is integrated into the rest of Cocoa so that you can use the features without having to learn a whole new paradigm of user interface design and building. In fact, you can get most of the benefits and features of Core Animation without having to leave the comfortable world of AppKit view-based user interface programming. During the first several chapters of this book, we will focus on what we can do with Core Animation with the tight integration of AppKit. Then, in the later chapters, we will focus on the features that we can create when we move to a purely Core Animation–based user interface.

Chapter 2, *Cocoa Animation*, on page 9 begins our journey into animated applications with a discussion of what is possible using only Cocoa APIs. The flow of the book takes you from familiar concepts in AppKit and slowly introduces the additional APIs that are part of the Core Animation framework. The chapters start with pure AppKit animation and then introduce the Core Animation APIs that are directly integrated into the AppKit. Finally, the book discusses the additional features we gain by using a "pure" Core Animation layer-based UI. The gradual introduction has two purposes. The first motivation is to transition from known concepts into the unknown by tying together concepts that are familiar and showing the unfamiliar in terms of the familiar. The second motivation is to show you what is possible without having to learn the whole Core Animation framework. For example, it is amazing how much is possible by simply turning on layer backing. Simply by calling one method, we can gain a huge amount of animation power, and we don't even have to really learn Core Animation. We can gradually move into it as the need arises instead of having to wrap our heads around a whole new framework just to get started.

I don't want to give the impression, however, that Core Animation is hard to learn. It's actually quite easy to pick up once you learn a few basic concepts. And although a lot of animation is possible in the Cocoa APIs, we gain a lot of flexibility and features as we start to use the Core Animation APIs. Chapter 3, *Animation Types*, on page 21 introduces the various types of animations that are available in the Core Animation framework.

Next up, Chapter 4, *Animation Timing*, on page 39 discusses the Core Animation classes related to controlling the timing of the animations that we use. Both of these chapters take an AppKit-centric approach to the material, and the examples are purely view-based. Again, this is to make the transition gradual. Once learned, though, the concepts are transferable directly to Core Animation layer-based animations.

Chapter 5, *Layer-Backed Views*, on page 53 discusses the new features we gain by turning on layer backing for our views. In this chapter, we begin to see some of the features that are possible with Core Animation layers, but again we stay mostly focused on the AppKit-centric view of things. But we are beginning our transition into a more Core Animation–focused user interface.

In Chapter 6, *Filtered Views*, on page 63, we see Core Image filters in action (Core Image is Apple's way of doing image processing on the GPU). Specifically, we will see how to apply any one of the dozens of Core Image filters that are available to our views. This chapter completes the look at what is possible with the Core Animation and AppKit integration. The next chapter (Chapter 7, *Core Animation*, on page 77) covers Core Animation–based user interfaces and the layer tree.

In Chapter 8, *Core Animation Layers*, on page 93, we see the way we would apply what we've already learned about Core Animation classes (in Chapter 3, *Animation Types*, on page 21; Chapter 4, *Animation Timing*, on page 39; Chapter 5, *Layer-Backed Views*, on page 53; and Chapter 6, *Filtered Views*, on page 63) and then apply this knowledge to layers. The chapter covers how layers work and what they have been doing for us in the previous chapters without us having to think about it.

In Chapter 9, *Layer Scrolling and Geometry*, on page 115, we explore the geometry of layers and see how to scroll them. You will learn the similarities and differences between the way AppKit scrolls views and be able to apply what you already know to learning layer scrolling.

In Chapter 10, *Layers in 3D*, on page 131, we explore how to animate layers in 3D, including building our own custom layer manager and making that take care of the heavy lifting for us so that our application and layer manipulation code can remain simple.

Next up, in Chapter 11, *Media Layers*, on page 147, we explore how to use various media types in a mixed UI based on layers. Core Animation allows us to mix and match media content of various types freely. For example, we can have a QuickTime movie playing in the same view as an OpenGL animation and place a Quartz Composer composition in the background. This mix-and-match approach opens many UI avenues that were just not possible before Core Animation.

Finally, the book ends by covering Core Animation for the iPhone (Chapter 12, *Core Animation on the iPhone*, on page 163). In this final chapter, we cover the various differences between developing for the iPhone and developing for Mac OS X. The good thing is that Core Animation is for the most part the same on the iPhone, so all the stuff you've learned applies with just a few caveats. This final chapter explains those caveats and teaches you some additional tricks about doing Core Animation on the iPhone.

Once you are done reading this book, there many Apple publications that you'll find helpful. Start with Apple's "Introduction to Core Animation Programming Guide" [App08a]. You'll next want to learn more in general about Core Image from the "Introduction to Core Image Programming Guide" [App08b]. Read more about the effects you can add to your animations in their "Introduction to Quartz Composer User Guide" [App07b]. You'll learn about working with 3D animations in the "OpenGL Programming Guide for Mac OS X" [App08c]. If you're sticking with two dimensions you'll enjoy the "Introduction to Quartz 2D Programming Guide" [App07a]. Finally, you can improve on your performance by reading the "Cocoa Drawing Tips" [App06].

1.3 Acknowledgments

Most acknowledgment sections have something to say like "making a book is a huge undertaking," and that is very true. But, somehow that just does not do the undertaking justice. You start with a simple thought or a brief conversation, and before you know it, your life is consumed in getting your thoughts organized and written.

This book started simply enough. At JavaOne in 2007, I ran into Daniel and mentioned that I was thinking of leaving the Java space for the OS X space. He mentioned that he was thinking of getting some OS X books going and that we should talk. A few weeks later, I began the adventure that became this book. So thanks, Daniel, one for getting me into this and two for turning my random passive prose into something that people can actually understand.

The people who gave up many hours of free time to help technically review the book also need a warm thanks. This book is much more accurate and coherently organized because of their input. So, in no particular order, Tim Wood, Bill Shirley, Dylan McNamee, Jason Jobe, Daniel Jalkut, Antonio Nunes, Eric Wing, Scott Stevenson, and Chris Adamson, thank you. These people really dug deep into the content and provided inestimable feedback on the accuracy, order, and organization of the book. It is a much better book for their involvement. The folks who provided feedback in the errata were also very helpful in finding technical errors and many other things that made the book much better—thanks!

Finally, I'd like to thank a 2,000-year-old carpenter for making my life more than I could have ever hoped or imagined.

You can find the code on the book's website. The code is organized by chapter, and each project is organized with Xcode so you can download double-click and follow along. Also, take a look at the screencasts for Core Animation at http://www.pragprog.com/screencasts/v-bdcora/. The screencasts offer a different approach to learning this material. They approach the topic starting from Core Animation instead of starting with AppKit. And the visual nature of them allows us to see the animations together as we build out the application in this book.

Finally, a note about the content and focus of this book: As Edison said, junk and imagination are required to invent. Junk is the raw material of a great invention; to the uninitiated or uninspired, the junk is useless, but to the person with imagination and knowledge, the junk is an invention waiting to be born. This book focuses on helping you understand the raw materials that you have to work with in Core Animation. Instead of trying to be your imagination, I attempt to spark your imagination. Often examples are contrived specifically to illustrate how something works or fits together rather than because they are a good fit for any particular application. I often choose the less-used effects or items to illustrate a point to try to spark your imagination toward other

options. Core Animation is new, and we as a community need to experiment with it to arrive at the "best" way to use it. Is the Ripple effect
the best way to show the introduction of a new item in the Dashboard?
Who knows? It looks really cool, but you might have a better idea. We
need to spend some time with this new framework building stuff that
is gaudy and crazy to push the limits of what is possible, and then we
will have honed our imaginations to understand this new mound of raw
materials that we have. So, as you go through the book, my hope is that
your imagination is sparked to invent something amazing.

The way to get started is to quit talking and begin doing.
► Walt Disney

Chapter 2

Cocoa Animation

In a world without animation, when you clicked a window's Minimize button, the window would just disappear, and a smaller version would instantly appear in the Dock. The move would happen so fast that you might think you had dismissed the window by clicking the Close button by mistake. Or you may realize you had clicked the Minimize button but not know where the window went. Add a little bit of animation, and you can see the window shrink and insert itself in a particular location on the Dock. The animation isn't just entertaining; it is directing your eye to the new location of the minimized window.

In this chapter, we'll see a simplified version of this action. First an image will instantaneously shrink and be moved to the middle of the right side of the screen. Then we will change a single line of code to animate the effect using the animator proxy. This example will show how to implement the simplest of animations and allow us to play with the "before" and "after" versions to begin to understand how judiciously adding animation can enrich our user interfaces.

2.1 Moving Without Animation

Our first example mimics a part of the action of minimizing a window to the Dock. We'll start with a picture in the lower-left corner of a window. When you press any key, the picture will shrink and be anchored to the middle of the right side of the window. There's no animation here.

In Figure 2.1, on the next page, we can see the two positions of the picture. As you repeatedly press the key, the picture jumps back and forth from side to side.

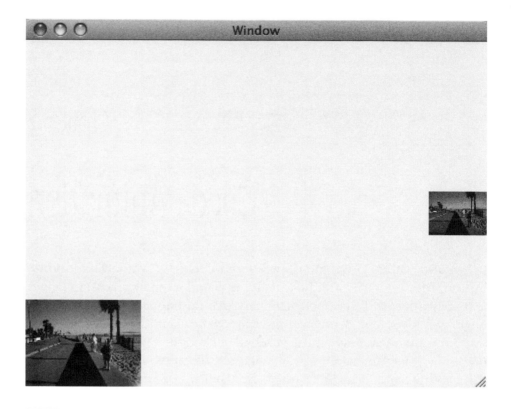

Figure 2.1: INITIAL AND FINAL IMAGE LOCATIONS

Setting Up the Window

You'll find an Xcode project and the necessary files in your code folder at code/CocoaAnimation/FirstAnimation/FirstAnimation.xcodeproj. Take a look at the NIB file, and you'll see a single window that contains a BaseView object.

As you'll see in the following code snippet from the custom view class, three steps are required to initialize this BaseView object:

1. Initialize the two rectangles required for the starting and ending positions for the image in line 4.
2. Add the image to the NSImageView that will be moved back and forth between these locations in line 5.
3. Add this NSImageView to the BaseView so that we can see the action in line 6.

CocoaAnimation/FirstAnimation/BaseView.m

```
Line 1    - (id)initWithFrame:(NSRect)frame {
  -           self = [super initWithFrame:frame];
  -           if (self) {
  -                       [self initializeFramePositions];
  5                       [self addImageToSubview];
  -                       [self addSubview:mover];
  -               }
  -           return self;
  -     }
```

You will also need to override the following two methods to handle keyboard events:

CocoaAnimation/FirstAnimation/BaseView.m

```
Line 1    - (BOOL)acceptsFirstResponder {
  -           return YES;
  -     }
  -
  5    - (void)keyDown:(NSEvent *)event {
  -               [self move];
  -     }
```

Returning YES from the acceptsFirstResponder method allows this view to be the first Responder in the responder chain, and thus it will get the first chance to respond to the key press events. We haven't done anything fancy with the keyDown: method. No matter what key is pressed, the application will respond by calling the move method. Now let's look at the details of moving the picture.

Setting the Beginning and Ending Positions

We'll use the NSMakeRect() function to create two rectangles: one for the initial position in the lower-left corner and a smaller one in the center of the right side of the window. The method takes four floating-point values as CGFloats. The first pair specifies the x and y values of the lower-left corner of the rectangle. The second pair specifies the width and height values of the rectangle.

The initializeFramePositions method creates a rectangle that is one quarter the width and one quarter the height of the containing window that is anchored in the lower-left corner. It also creates a rectangle one half that size anchored to the middle of the right side of the window.

CocoaAnimation/FirstAnimation/BaseView.m

```
-(void)initializeFramePositions {
        CGFloat  frameX = NSWidth([self frame]);
        CGFloat  frameY = NSHeight([self frame]);

        leftFramePosition = NSMakeRect(0.0f, 0.0f, frameX / 4.0f,
                                       frameY / 4.0f);
        rightFramePosition = NSMakeRect(7.0f * frameX / 8.0f,
                                        7.0f *frameY / 16.0f,
                                        frameX / 8.0f, frameY/ 8.0f);

        mover = [[NSImageView alloc] initWithFrame:leftFramePosition];
        isRight = NO;
}

-(void)addImageToSubview {
        [mover setImageScaling:NSScaleToFit];
        [mover setImage:[NSImage imageNamed:@"photo.jpg"]];
}
```

The addImageToSubview method is included for completeness. This is where the image is linked to the NSImageView.

Moving the Image

Now that we've set the stage, it is surprisingly easy to move the image. You just check whether the image is on the left or the right side and move it to the other side by passing the NSImageView the rectangle corresponding to its target position.

CocoaAnimation/FirstAnimation/BaseView.m

```
Line 1  - (void)move {
          if(isRight) {
            [mover setFrame:leftFramePosition];
          } else {
    5       [mover setFrame:rightFramePosition];
          }
              isRight = !isRight;
        }
```

Build and run the application, and press any key on the keyboard to see the picture jump back and forth between the two positions.

2.2 Introducing Cocoa Animation

In this section, you'll see how easy it is to add animation to an application. You just saw an application that moved a view around without any animation. Let's take that same application and animate it. Of course, this is just the beginning. There's plenty left to learn, but let's start with the simplest of animations.

Smooth Moves

There needs to be only one small change to the code to animate the movement you saw in the previous section. Instead of sending the set-Frame message to the NSImageView object called mover, you first ask mover for its animator, and you then send setFrame: to that instead.

```
- (void)move {
    if(isRight) {
        [[mover animator] setFrame:leftFramePosition];
    } else {
        [[mover animator] setFrame:rightFramePosition];
    }
    isRight = !isRight;
}
```

Take a second to make this small change to the code, and run the application. The image now smoothly animates between its initial state and the docked state. We will cover the animator in detail shortly in Section 2.3, *Animation and the Animator Proxy*, on page 15.

Not only does this look fantastic as a visual treatment, but it also adds to the user experience. The user can see what the application is doing with the picture. In our very simple application here, it's of course obvious what is happening with the picture, but in a more elaborate application, the new location and minimization of the picture might not be nearly as obvious. The animation provides additional visual cues to the user about what is going on with their content.

Beautiful, functional, and simple—all we had to do was invoke methods on the animator instead of the view directly. Animation with no threads and no synchronization!

Simplification of Animation

Animation isn't new. What's new is that now it is easy for you to animate various aspects of your user interface. In the past, we as developers had to make a cached representation of a view and then take that cached representation and move it around on the screen via an alternate thread, making sure all the while to manage concurrent access to data structures. Although this approach could yield some nice-looking results, the underlying code often becomes a bear to maintain because it's so complex.

Applying Your Animations

As you learn each new animation technique in this book, it's a good idea to consider when you might want to and might not want to use it. In this first application, you are adding the simplest of animations to allow a user's eye to easily follow an affine transformation. Apple uses a technique similar to this when reducing windows to the Dock, when displaying the sidebar in the Preview application, and when all windows currently on the desktop are displayed using Expose.

So, when might you *not* want to use an animation? Well, as an example, you may want to clear the desktop of all windows not owned by the current active application. From the Application menu, you can select Hide Others, and the documents belonging to other applications will instantaneously disappear. There is no animation on the desktop (although there is an animation that accompanies this action in the Dock). Animating the background windows might look cool, but since the user is interested in the active application and not the background applications, the animation would simply be eye candy.

The decision should always boil down to whether an animation will assist the user. Never include an animation to show off your own skills.

With the animator proxy (which we will cover in detail in the next section), you can animate your views and windows without having to learn a new framework or anything about threads or locks. I'll go into more detail on the animator proxy, but for now the most important thing to know is that the proxy looks to our code just like the object under it. You don't have to learn any of the details of how to implement animation yourself. It is all encapsulated behind the animator. And, since you already know the NSView and NSWindow classes, adding animation is as simple as asking for the animator proxy and then using the proxy exactly as you would the window or view. The proxy will then animate the state changes for you. As you'll learn, it is amazingly simple to perform many sophisticated animation techniques using what amounts to a half line of code.

We can build on this animation and make it a lot more complex, but first let's look in detail at what is happening behind this really simple half line of code that we added to our example to get the picture to animate across the screen instead of jump. Specifically, we will see the proxy and how it finds and invokes the animation objects that make adding animation to our applications so easy.

2.3 Animation and the Animator Proxy

As we have seen, the animation of Cocoa classes is performed through a proxy object that we get by calling the animator method. In this section, we are going to look at what this proxy is, how it works, and how the animator finds the animations to be performed. We will also see how default animations are set up for custom properties of NSView subclasses.

The animator proxy comes from a new protocol called NSAnimatablePropertyContainer, introduced with Leopard (currently only NSWindow and NSView conform) as part of AppKit. This protocol allows objects to have their property changes animated instead of the change being instantaneous. You use the animator method to get to the proxy and send it a message to get the animation behavior discussed earlier. For now, we will be using this method only, but we'll discuss the remainder of the protocol in detail later when we look at customizing the animations.

Finding Animations

The animator proxy creates, configures, and kicks off the animations when any of the properties that can be animated are changed. When a set method is invoked on the proxy (like setFrame: in our earlier example), the animator performs a search for the animation object to invoke. In Figure 2.2, on the next page, we can see the basic message flow the animator uses. First it calls the animationForKey: method with the key that is being changed (in our example frame would be used). animationForKey: first looks in the receiver's animations dictionary, and if an animation is found, it is returned. (We will eventually be adding custom animations to this dictionary in Chapter 3, *Animation Types*, on page 21.) If not, then the class method defaultAnimationForKey: is called, and that animation is returned. The proxy then invokes the animation, which in turn animates the change for the property.

If nil is returned from animationForKey:, then the change in the property is not animated; instead, the value is simply passed to the underlying object.

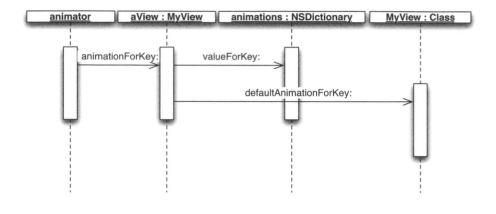

Figure 2.2: FINDING THE ANIMATION TO INVOKE

The default animation is a CABasicAnimation that does a basic linear interpolation between the fromValue and the toValue. By default, the current value of the changing property is used as the from value, and the new value is used as the toValue for the animation. The animator then passes responsibility to an instance of CAAnimation for doing the interpolation between the fromValue and toValue and animating these changes. We will discuss more about the way animations work and the other choices we have in Chapter 3, *Animation Types*, on page 21.

Keep in mind that the animator proxy is simply finding an animation and then invoking it. As we move into our discussion of animation objects, remember the process that the animator uses to find the animations. We will take advantage of this process to eventually attach our own animations to our views and windows to create our own custom animation effects.

2.4 Animation and Interpolation

As we just discussed, once an animation object is found, it is used to animate the property that is being changed. The animation *interpolates* between the fromValue and toValue. By default, the fromValue is the current value of the property, and the toValue is the new value that was passed into the set method. The default interpolation is a straight line that starts at time zero and fromValue and finishes at the end time and toValue. Something important to keep in mind here is that Core Anima-

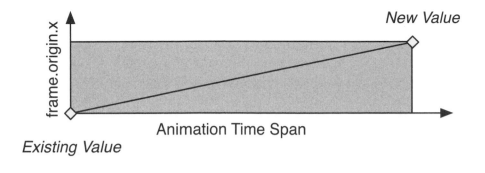

Figure 2.3: BASIC ANIMATION INTERPOLATION TIMELINE

tion is time-based, not frame-based. So even if the interpolation calls for thirty frames to be displayed to change a property from one value to another, if the hardware is able to display only fifteen of them in the allotted time, then only fifteen will be drawn. Core Animation is, of course, clever enough to still make the animation as smooth as possible, so intermittent frames, rather than a group of frames at either end of the animation, will be dropped.

When we invoke the setFrame: method on a view animator proxy as we did in our example, the default animation will use the existing value as the fromValue (the Existing Value in Figure 2.3). The value we pass into the setFrame: method is used as the toValue (the New Value in Figure 2.3). The default animation time span is 0.25 seconds, so in our example, the first point will be 0 seconds and the existing frame value; and the end point will be 0.25 seconds and the new frame value.

The animation object is responsible for doing the interpolation between the fromValue and the toValue and making that interpolation fit with the time span set for the animation. A typical refresh rate is sixty frames a second, so if we are going to move a view from point 1 along the x-axis to point 2 (for the example's sake and to make the math easy, let's use 0 and 10 as our two x values) in the default 0.25 seconds, we will need fifteen locations (0.25 * 60). So, we need to calculate the value for x along the line between the first point and the second point for each of the thirteen locations between 0.0 seconds and 0.25 seconds that we don't know (that is, we know the 0 location and the 0.25 location as the from and to values).

Another way to think of it is that our first point is the time at 0.0 seconds and x at 0.0, and the final point is the time at 0.25 seconds and x at 10.0. We need to find the thirteen locations between these two points that we will show for our animation; 0.25 divided by 15 is 0.016667, so that is the increment between each time point. Now we need to find the x value for each frame. That is done by calculating the slope of the line (also known as the *rise over the run*). This is easy to calculate by simply dividing 10 by 0.25, which yields 40.

Now we can multiply our time points by 40 to get the value of x along the line (in other words, our formula is x = 40 * time + start time; also keep in mind that the x value runs vertically, which is typically what we think of as the y-axis). The points would be (t = 0, x = 0), (t = 0.01667, x = 0.66668), (t = 0.03334, x = 1.33334). . . to (t = 0.25, x = 10.0). That gives us the value of x and t for each frame in our animation.

The math of doing interpolation can become quite tedious, and thankfully we don't have to mess with it, because the animation objects take care of it for us. The only important thing to remember is the basic concept of what is being done for you. I often find that understanding these kinds of details can help me figure out a bug either in my code or in my understanding and can help me figure out why an unexpected behavior has happened.

We aren't restricted to using only straight lines for our interpolation. A straight line corresponds to the case in which we are moving from start to finish at a constant speed. Several types of curves are available to use when we are doing animation. We will discuss them in detail in Chapter 3, *Animation Types*, on page 21, coming up next.

Regardless of the curve type we choose, the animation object understands how to interpolate between values of many different kinds, and simple values such as float and double are supported. But more complex types such as NSPoint, NSSize, and NSRect are supported as well. The animator will do a reasonable job of defaulting the animation between two different values for any of the attributes of a view that are of these types. We have already seen this in the earlier example of moving the picture across its superview. We simply set a new frame rectangle, and the image was animated to its new spot on the screen. In fact, any property that is one of these types (double, float, NSPoint, NSSize, or NSRect) can be animated.

Some properties of these types (alphaValue, for example) must have layer backing turned on to function. We will talk more about the layer-backed properties in Chapter 5, *Layer-Backed Views*, on page 53.

In this chapter, we discussed the basics of Cocoa Animation and saw how the animator proxy works. Armed with just this knowledge, we are able to produce some fairly interesting behaviors in our user interfaces. But we have only just begun to see what is possible; there is a lot of great stuff yet to come.

In Chapter 3, *Animation Types*, on page 21, we will see an example of adding an Ease-In curve to an animation as we discuss the various types of animations that come with Core Animation as well as learn how to customize their behavior.

The aim, if reached or not, makes great the life: Try to be
Shakespeare, leave the rest to fate!
► Robert Browning

Chapter 3

Animation Types

In the previous chapter, we saw how easy it is to add a default animation to our applications. Even this type of animation looks great, but we don't have much control. All we can do is set a new value and watch what happens. In this chapter, we are going to dig into part of what is going on behind the scenes so that we can get precisely the animation we want.

Up to this point, we have seen only AppKit APIs, but in this chapter we are going to start to mix in the animation classes from Core Animation. The animation classes are tightly integrated into AppKit, which makes it possible for us to use much of Core Animation without having to get into the details of the whole framework. The animation classes give us a great deal of control over what our effects look like and how they play out onscreen.

3.1 Basic Animation

In the example in Section 2.3, *Finding Animations*, on page 15, we saw the CABasicAnimation class in action. This basic animation was responsible for the smooth transition from the left to the right of the screen. The basic animation is just that: basic. We can use it for all the simple stuff that you don't want to think too much about. When we are simply moving a view from one side of the screen to the other or scaling the view (we did both in the previous example, if you recall), we can leave everything to the defaults to get the basic animation.

For many of the things you want to animate, this animation fits the bill because it's easy to use since every property has reasonable defaults. However, easy does not always lead to the effect you want. Several other types of animations have more advanced capabilities that we can exploit to make some truly fantastic-looking (and functional) user interfaces. Let's dig into the other animations types now.

3.2 Keyframe Animations

Placing an animated item precisely where we want it when we want it to be there takes more than a basic animation. That kind of functionality is accomplished by using the keyframe animation. With it we can specify exactly what value we want our animated property to have and exactly the length of time we want the property to take to reach that value.

The term *keyframe* comes from the animation and motion graphics world (and should not be confused with the *key* term used with key-value coding). If you are familiar with Apple's Final Cut Studio suite, which includes Motion and Final Cut Pro, you have probably played with keyframes. If not, a keyframe is basically a reference point around which interpolation happens. The keyframe specifies a point in the animation that is precise and does not depend on an interpolation function. In a program like Motion, you create a keyframe by specifying a location and a time, and Motion takes care of interpolating the "before" and "after" sequence. If you specify multiple keyframes, then Motion will interpolate between each of them, making sure to hit your specific locations at the specified time. In Core Animation, we do basically the same thing; we specify a value at a time, and Core Animation will interpolate between the keyframes.

Let's say we want the opacity of an image to fade from zero to 75% and then back down to zero over the course of an animation (in other words, the image fades in and then fades back out). In addition, we also want the opacity to remain zero until 25% of the time has passed and then be back at zero when 75% of the time has passed. The only way to make this happen is with a keyframe animation.

The curve is shown in Figure 3.1, on the facing page. The horizontal axis is the time span, and the vertical axis is the opacity. The initial diamond is the point in time where the image starts to fade in, and then until the next diamond, the opacity is smoothly increasing. Then as the animation hits that second point, the opacity begins to decrease until the animation finishes at the final diamond back at zero opacity.

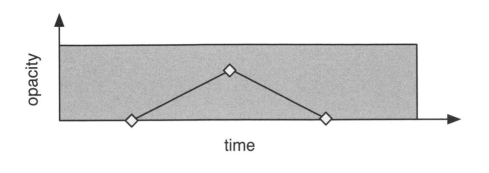

Figure 3.1: OPACITY KEYFRAME EXAMPLE

Keyframes are specified by providing an array of values, one value for each specific keyframe we want to set during the animation. For example, each of the diamonds in Figure 3.1 is a keyframe for opacity, with the opacity values being (0.0, 0.75, 0.0).

Another important thing to keep in mind about keyframe animations is that they work in terms of "normalized" time. The total duration of the keyframe animation is specified in seconds, but the keyframe begin and end points are specified as percentages of the total duration. The beginning of time for the animation is 0, and the end of time is 1. So, we can think of points in time as a percentage of completion. In other words, 0.5 is half of the time frame for the animation, regardless of how long it really runs.

Let's consider further changing the opacity as in the graph in Figure 3.1. The array of values, as we said, are (0.0, 0.75, 0.0), and the time values are (0.25, 0.50, 0.75).

At the beginning of the animation, the alpha value is 0.0, and the value remains at zero until the animation arrives at 25% of its duration. Between 25% of the duration and 50% of the duration, the opacity will continue to rise smoothly until the duration reaches 50%. At that point, the opacity will be 75%, and 50% of the duration will have elapsed. As the animation proceeds to 75% of its duration, the opacity will fade back to 0% where it will remain through the final 25% of the duration.

Keyframes in Keynote

One of the new features in Keynote 4 (for iWork '08) is to animate objects along a path. One demo during the intro of the new version shows an airplane moving along a curved bezier path. The CAKeyframeAnimation class is intended to allow us to build that very same kind of animation into our applications.

The code to create the keyframe animation would look like this:

```
- (CAKeyframeAnimation *)opacityAnimation {
    CAKeyframeAnimation *animation = [CAKeyframeAnimation animation];
    animation.values = [NSArray arrayWithObjects:
                        [NSNumber numberWithFloat:0.0],
                        [NSNumber numberWithFloat:0.75],
                        [NSNumber numberWithFloat:0.0], nil];
    animation.keyTimes = [NSArray arrayWithObjects:
                        [NSNumber numberWithFloat:0.25],
                        [NSNumber numberWithFloat:0.50],
                        [NSNumber numberWithFloat:0.75], nil];
    return animation;
}
```

One of the things we can do to eliminate some of the complexity and still get most of the control is to let the keyframe animation handle the timing. If we leave out setting the time values, the keyframe animation will just evenly distribute the values we provide over the time frame. If we provide three values, the first value is the starting value, the second value will be reached at 50% of the elapsed time, and the third value is at 100% of the time.

Keyframes and Paths

In addition to allowing you to set the *key values* along an animation keyframe, animations also allow you to use paths to animate dual-valued properties such as the position of a layer (position has both x and y values). For example, suppose we want to move a picture along a nonlinear path. All we have to do is create a path that plots the points precisely the way we want them and supply that to the animation. The path will then be used to determine values instead of an interpolation.

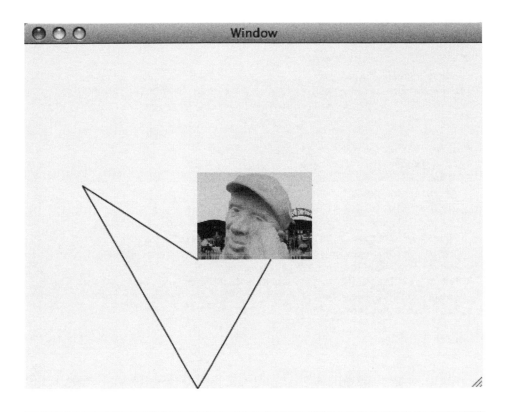

Figure 3.2: KEYFRAME MOVEMENT

The path technique will work only with dual-valued properties, that is, any property with two values. Basically, this is any property that is typed as NSPoint or NSSize. The x values in the path are used by the animation to change either the x value of the point or the width value of the size, and the y values correspond to the y value of the point or the height value of the size. The next example will show this in action.

We will use this technique to move a view around the screen with a keyframe animation. We will use an instance of CGPath to animate the frameOrigin property of the picture in the pointed heart shape shown in Figure 3.2. The picture moves across the screen following the path. The heart-shaped path that is used for the keyframing is also drawn in the background so we can see where the picture is and where it is headed.

Let's look at the code that makes all this happen:

AnimationTypes/KeyFrameMoveAView/KeyFrameView.m

```
Line 1   - (void)addBounceAnimation {
    -       [mover setAnimations:[NSDictionary dictionaryWithObjectsAndKeys:
    -                             self.originAnimation, @"frameOrigin", nil]];
    -     }
    5
    -     - (id)initWithFrame:(NSRect)frame {
    -       self = [super initWithFrame:frame];
    -       if (self) {
    -         // inset by 3/8's
   10         CGFloat xInset = 3.0f * (NSWidth(frame) / 8.0f);
    -         CGFloat yInset = 3.0f * (NSHeight(frame) / 8.0f);
    -         NSRect moverFrame = NSInsetRect(frame, xInset, yInset);
    -         mover = [[NSImageView alloc] initWithFrame:moverFrame];
    -         [mover setImageScaling:NSScaleToFit];
   15         [mover setImage:[NSImage imageNamed:@"photo.jpg"]];
    -         [self addSubview:mover];
    -         [self addBounceAnimation];
    -       }
    -       return self;
   20     }
```

In this first bit of code, we are initializing the mover view (the NSIm-ageView that holds our picture) to the center of the screen, and then on line 17 we add the animation to the view. Recall from Section 2.3, *Finding Animations*, on page 15 that adding an animation to the animations dictionary will place our custom animation in the search path. This of course will cause our animation to be used instead of the default. Next let's look at the animation creation code:

AnimationTypes/KeyFrameMoveAView/KeyFrameView.m

```
Line 1   - (CAKeyframeAnimation *)originAnimation {
    -       CAKeyframeAnimation *originAnimation = [CAKeyframeAnimation animation];
    -       originAnimation.path = self.heartPath;
    -       originAnimation.duration = 2.0f;
    5       originAnimation.calculationMode = kCAAnimationPaced;
    -       return originAnimation;
    -     }
```

We should pay attention to two parts of this code. First on line 3, we are setting the path to the animation. Recall that the animation will use the x and y values of this path as the x and y values of the frameOrigin for our moving view. The next thing to notice is on line 5, where we set the calculationMode property of the animation. Setting this value to kCAAni-mationPaced causes the animation to equally distribute the time across the whole path. By default, a keyframe animation will distribute the time equally across the path fragments so each path fragment would have the same amount of time to move the view along. This makes the long path fragments move the view quickly and the short segments move the view slowly. We've chosen instead to make our entire journey at a constant speed. Now let's look at the way to create the path:

AnimationTypes/KeyFrameMoveAView/KeyFrameView.m

```
- (CGPathRef)heartPath {
  NSRect frame = [mover frame];
  if(heartPath == NULL) {
    heartPath = CGPathCreateMutable();
    CGPathMoveToPoint(heartPath, NULL, NSMinX(frame), NSMinY(frame));
    CGPathAddLineToPoint(heartPath, NULL, NSMinX(frame) - NSWidth(frame),
                      NSMinY(frame) + NSHeight(frame) * 0.85);
    CGPathAddLineToPoint(heartPath, NULL, NSMinX(frame),
                      NSMinY(frame) - NSHeight(frame) * 1.5);
    CGPathAddLineToPoint(heartPath, NULL, NSMinX(frame) + NSWidth(frame),
                      NSMinY(frame) + NSHeight(frame) * 0.85);
    CGPathAddLineToPoint(heartPath, NULL, NSMinX(frame), NSMinY(frame));
    CGPathCloseSubpath(heartPath);
  }
  return heartPath;
}
```

This is very typical Quartz path creation code. If you want more information, look at [GL06]. Next up let's look at the animation code:

AnimationTypes/KeyFrameMoveAView/KeyFrameView.m

```
Line 1  - (void)bounce {
   -        NSRect rect = [mover frame];
   -        [[mover animator] setFrameOrigin:rect.origin];
   -      }
```

It's fairly simple code here too. All we do is call the setFrameOrigin: method on our moving view, and the animation takes care of the rest (bounce is called from keyDown: when any key is hit). Recall that since we have added an animation to the animations dictionary under the frameOrigin key, the animator will find it during its search and use ours instead of the default animation. Also notice that we are setting the frame origin with its current value. Since we want the animation to end up back where it started, this is expected. If we wanted to have the view animate along a path to another location, we'd set that new location here. But we would have to be careful to make sure the path's final point matches with the destination we set; otherwise, we'd get a choppy animation. You can find more detail on this later in Section 3.5, *Custom Animation and Interpolation*, on page 36.

As you can see, keyframe animations give us a very fine-grained level of control over the various properties we seek to animate. We can specify as many intermediate points as needed to achieve the effect we want. We also have complete control over the time intervals spent for each section of our path.

3.3 Grouping Animations

Animations can be grouped and then triggered with the change of a single attribute. For example, we could group an alpha fade, a frame movement, and a resize. Then add the group animation to the view so that it is triggered when the frame origin is set.

When working with groups, you need to set the keyPath for each of the animations that is part of the group. The group is added (not the individual animation objects) to the animations dictionary so it is discovered and run as discussed in Section 2.3, *Finding Animations*, on page 15. However, the constituent animations are not associated with any particular key (since they are in the group and not part of the animations dictionary) and thus will not cause any animation. So, we need to set their keyPaths. To do that, we can use animationWithKeyPath: at animation creation time, or we can set the keyPath property after creation. Don't worry if this is not crystal clear right now; you will see in the example how to set this up.

Another interesting point about the keys an animation is associated with is that they do not have to be associated with a key on the view they are animating. The animation is associated with a keyPath, so the animation can affect anything that is reachable from the view via a keyPath. For the typical use, we will be using a simple key (frameOrigin, frameSize, and so on), but when we start looking at filters later in Chapter 7, *Core Animation*, on page 77, we will use the keyPath to animate the properties of the filter.

Any of the animations we've seen thus far can be put into groups. The combinations of what is possible are almost endless. We can even put a group into another group and have lots and lots of animations happening at the same time. Of course, we have to temper our imaginations by making sure that the animation is useful and not just eye candy.

Here's an example of nesting animations into a group in which we rotate and enlarge a picture. It starts at the center of the screen, grows and rotates, and then returns to its original position.

Eye Candy and Animations

Although it's nice to have eye candy, if an effect does not provide a real benefit to the user, it will eventually become irritating. So when you are putting animations into your application, make sure there is a valid user need being met. Eye candy that meets a need will be shown off; eye candy that is simply flash will eventually be ignored or turned off.

In Figure 3.3, on the following page, we see both frames of the animation, namely, the "before" and "after" frames.

Let's dive into the code that makes this grouped animation work. Here is the code for the initWithFrame: method:

AnimationTypes/GroupAnimation/GroupAnimationView.m

```
Line 1   - (id)initWithFrame:(NSRect)frame {
    -       self = [super initWithFrame:frame];
    -       if (self) {
    -         // inset by 3/8's
    5         CGFloat xInset = 3.0f * (NSWidth(frame) / 8.0f);
    -         CGFloat yInset = 3.0f * (NSHeight(frame) / 8.0f);
    -         NSRect moverFrame = NSInsetRect(frame, xInset, yInset);
    -         moverFrame.origin.x = NSMidX([self bounds]) -
    -           (NSWidth(moverFrame) / 2.0f);
   10         moverFrame.origin.y = NSMidY([self bounds]) -
    -           (NSHeight(moverFrame) / 2.0f);
    -         mover = [[NSImageView alloc] initWithFrame:moverFrame];
    -         [mover setImageScaling:NSScaleToFit];
    -         [mover setImage:[NSImage imageNamed:@"photo.jpg"]];
   15         NSDictionary *animations =
    -           [NSDictionary dictionaryWithObjectsAndKeys:
    -            [self groupAnimation:moverFrame], @"frameRotation", nil];
    -         [mover setAnimations:animations];
    -         [self addSubview:mover];
   20       }
    -       return self;
    -     }
```

The initWithFrame: is similar to the other initWithFrame: methods we have seen in past examples. On line 18, we are specifying the animations dictionary for the view as we have in earlier examples, but we are adding a group instead of a single animation (we will see the individual animation creation shortly). We have tied the group to the frameRotation key, which will cause our group to be used instead of the default animation

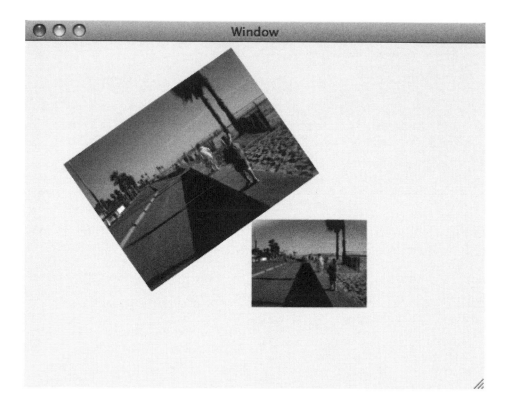

Figure 3.3: GROUP ANIMATION FRAMES

when the frameRotation property is changed. Next let's look at the code that we use to create the constituent animations:

AnimationTypes/GroupAnimation/GroupAnimationView.m

```
Line 1  - (CAAnimation *)frameAnimation:(NSRect)aniFrame {
          CAKeyframeAnimation *frameAnimation =
          [CAKeyframeAnimation animationWithKeyPath:@"frame"];
          NSRect start = aniFrame;
     5    NSRect end = NSInsetRect(aniFrame, -NSWidth(start) * 0.50,
                                  -NSHeight(start) * 0.50);
          frameAnimation.values = [NSArray arrayWithObjects:
                                  [NSValue valueWithRect:start],
                                  [NSValue valueWithRect:end], nil];
     10   return frameAnimation;
          }

          - (CABasicAnimation *)rotationAnimation {
          CABasicAnimation *rotation =
     15   [CABasicAnimation animationWithKeyPath:@"frameRotation"];
```

```
     rotation.fromValue = [NSNumber numberWithFloat:0.0f];
     rotation.toValue = [NSNumber numberWithFloat:45.0f];
     return rotation;
   }

   - (CAAnimationGroup *)groupAnimation:(NSRect)frame {
     CAAnimationGroup *group = [CAAnimationGroup animation];
     group.animations = [NSArray arrayWithObjects:
                           [self frameAnimation:frame],
                           [self rotationAnimation], nil];
     group.duration = 1.0f;
     group.autoreverses = YES;
     return group;
   }
```

The groupAnimation: method on line 21 creates the group and configures it so that it can be put into the animations dictionary of the mover view. We set the animations array to the two animations we discussed earlier (rotation and size change). We also set the duration to one second and then set the animation to autoreverse. We discussed the duration earlier, so let's get into the autoreverses property. Setting this property to YES tells the animation to reverse the animation after it's finished so that the property values finish where they started.

The group assumes all the responsibilities of the animations in the group except for animating the actual property to which the contained animation is tied. In other words, since we set the duration and autoreverse properties on the group in the example, the group will control the timing of its constituents. Or another way to think of it is that if one of the contained animations were to set the autoreverses property to NO, it would be ignored in favor of the setting on the group.

Another important aspect to keep in mind while putting your animations into groups is that their delegate is not called when the animation is run as part of a group. So if we were to set a delegate on the frameSize animation, it would not be called since that animation is in a group.

On line 1, we see the frameAnimation: method. This creates a keyframe animation and sets the values to start at the existing frame and then swell to 1.5 times as big. Since no time values are set (via the keyTimes property), the animation uses the default timing of simply spreading the change out equally over the animation's time span.

On line 13, we see the frameRotation animation being created. This is a simple animation object with its fromValue set to 0 degrees and a toValue

When to Group

Use grouped animations when you want to control the timing of two or more animations. One typical user interaction that would benefit is revealing detailed information about a selection. After a user has made a selection from a list, animating the details gives context, and if more than one animation is needed, then grouping them makes a lot of sense.

As an example, consider Front Row's display of your album list. As you scroll through the list, your album art is displayed on the left. If, however, you remain on a single album, the slightly rotated album art shrinks, it loses its perspective rotation, and the details (artist, genre, and so on) fade into the scene. Three animations are grouped together here: the rotation, shrinking, and text fade. I have no idea how Front Row implements this feature (it predates Core Animation), but we could re-create it with a group that contains these three animations.

of 45 degrees. Since the group is set to autoreverse, the rotation will go from 0 to 45 and back to 0.

And finally let's take a quick look at the event-handling code:

AnimationTypes/GroupAnimation/GroupAnimationView.m

```
- (BOOL)acceptsFirstResponder {
  return YES;
}

- (void)keyDown:(NSEvent *)event {
  [[mover animator] setFrameRotation:[mover frameRotation]];
}
```

In the keyDown: method, we are simply invoking the change by asking the animator to set the frameRotation: to the initial value whenever the user hits any key. You might notice that if you hold down a key or hit one during the animation, then the results might not match your expectations. We discussed this in more detail on page 27.

Grouped animations are a great way to add sophisticated animations to our applications. We can add any number of animations to a single group, but we also must be careful to make sure what we do in that regard is something our users would want to see again and again.

3.4 Animating Transitions

As subviews are added or removed, their appearance or disappearance can be animated via a transition. You might not think of a cross-fade as an animation, but you are essentially animating one image's opacity to increase in the same location as another image's opacity is decreasing. The CATransition class makes it possible. Transitions provide great feedback to our users. As items come and go from a view, we can animate their arrival or departure so that the users can see exactly what is happening.

The default transition is a cross-fade; however, several other transitions are included. We can also use any Core Image transition we'd like. This can make for some very exciting animations that can truly help our users understand what is happening with the application. For the transitions to work, however, we must turn on layer backing (which is done for you in the example). We will go into the details of layer backing in Chapter 5, *Layer-Backed Views*, on page 53.

To show the transitions in action, we have another simple example. In this example, we have two image views that we will transition between by hitting the 'r' key. In Figure 3.4, on the next page, we see the middle of the transition taking place between the beach and the snowman.

Now let's take a look at what you have to do in the code to make this happen:

`AnimationTypes/Transition/TransitionView.m`

```
Line 1   - (void)keyDown:(NSEvent *)event {
             if(nil != [self.beach superview]) {
               [[self animator] replaceSubview:self.beach with:self.snow];
             } else if(nil != [self.snow superview]) {
      5        [[self animator] replaceSubview:self.snow with:self.beach];
             }
         }
```

All you have to do is to call the animator and ask it to replace one subview with another, and you get a nice cross-fade transition. It's amazingly simple.

Now, there is a bit of a trick here. As mentioned earlier, layer backing has to be turned on for the transitions to work properly. That has been done for you in the NIB file, though, so you don't have to mess with it. To see where this is switched on, choose the TransitionView in Interface Builder and hit Command+2 to see the animation inspector.

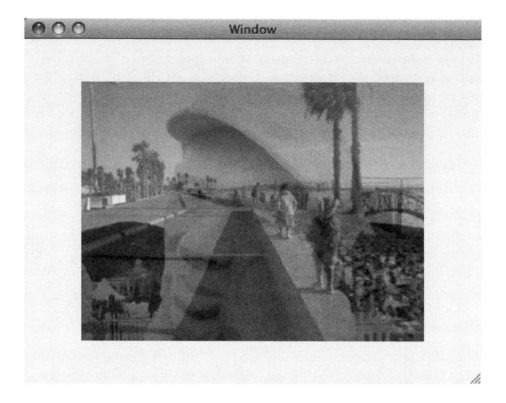

Figure 3.4: TRANSITION ANIMATION FRAME 2

By default, the animation is going to choose the cross-fade that we see in this example. But we can also specify (by adding a CATransition animation to the mover's animations dictionary under the subviews key) any one of the built-in animations. Here is the code to use to specify the Move In transition that animates from the top:

```
- (CATransition *)animation {
  CATransition *trans = [CATransition animation];
  trans.type = kCATransitionMoveIn;
  trans.subtype = kCATransitionFromTop;
  return trans;
}
```

We then simply have to add this transition to the animations dictionary of the view with self.animations = [NSDictionary dictionaryWithObject:[self animation] forKey:@"subviews"];, and we get a different transition.

Helpful Transitions

Transitions give the user cues about what is going on with the application. A major change in state or in interaction mode is a good place for a transition. Remember, though, that as with all animations, it's important to serve the needs of the user, not show off your ability to code transitions. As a concrete example of overblown transitions, think about all the keynote presentations you have seen. Some presenters take pride in stuffing every conceivable transition between slides into their presentations. Although many of the transitions look really cool, they become an annoyance; unless the transition conveys information, it's just plain irritating.

To solidify this, think about a presentation on how to transition from Carbon to Cocoa. The first part of the slide deck could present how something is done in Carbon, and then the transition into how to perform a similar task in Cocoa could have a Confetti transition. The transition shows additional information, and the presenter is "blowing up" the old way by teaching you the new way. If the Confetti transition were used between each slide, it would just become annoying.

The same principles work in our applications; we could do a Confetti-type transition between pages in a document, but after the first "oh, wow" moment, it's very likely that it would just be irritating to the user and get turned off (if we made that possible). By contrast, consider a cross-fade between pages in an inspector when the selection changes. That type of transition would actually help the user keep context. These are the types of transitions that we should be putting into our applications.

3.5 Custom Animation and Interpolation

When we use an animator to change the properties of a view or window, the property is changed according to the animator's interpolation function. The interpolation usually makes for a nice, smooth animation. If we use our own animations, however, we need to be careful to make sure the animation's initial value and the view's current value are the same. If they are not, we can get "choppiness" at the front or back of our animations. Of course, the easiest way to make sure everything is smooth is to not set the fromValue or toValue and let the animation get the values from the view.

The animation assumes (rightly) that the initial frame and final frame are "taken care of" by the current location and final location. So, as it's animating between the fromValue and the toValue, it does not interpolate between the current value of the property and the fromValue or in any other way try to ensure that the move from the first frame to the second frame of the animation is smooth.

For example, suppose we want to move a view from its original coordinates of (25.0, 25.0) to new coordinates of (125.0, 125.0). For this simple animation, we could use the animator directly, but for the sake of this illustration, let's create our own CABasicAnimation and make it the animation for the frameOrigin. If we specify the fromValue on the animation to anything but (25.0, 25.0), we will get choppy animation at the start. Of course, we'd never do this on purpose, but it is a common bug and worth thinking about as you write your animation code. We need to be careful when creating our own animations to take into account the initial and final state of the property so that we end up with a smooth animation.

To make this more concrete, consider our bouncing snowman from our earlier keyframe animation example. If you hit the B button during the animation, you might have noticed that the whole animation sort of acts strangely. Instead of ending up back in the center of the view where it started, the snowman goes through the whole path but then jumps to the spot you hit B. The "initial value" of position is no longer the first point in the path; instead, it is the location of the snowman when you hit the B key. In the bounce method (back on line 1, discussed on page 27), we set frameOrigin to its current value. Since there is an animation tied to the frameOrigin property, it is triggered, but that animation starts at the center of the view (the initial location of the view), so we get some jumping around at the end and beginning of the animation. Spend some time experimenting with this code to make it even more concrete.

We have seen the various types of animations that we can use to animate our user interfaces in this chapter. There are more details to cover, and we will get to them in Chapter 7, *Core Animation*, on page 77. For now keep in mind that we have lots of options to make our user interface elements animate. Now that we are experts on the kinds of animations that are possible, let's take a look at how to control the timing of our animations.

Computers are incredibly fast, accurate, and stupid.
Human beings are incredibly slow, inaccurate, and
brilliant. Together they are powerful beyond imagination.
▶ Albert Einstein

Chapter 4

Animation Timing

In Chapter 3, *Animation Types*, on page 21, we saw the types of animations we can use. Being able to change the animation type opened up a whole new set of options and allowed a greater level of control over how our objects animate. In this chapter, we'll learn to change the timing of our animations by manipulating the timing curve used by animations. This allows us to change the feel of our application. For example, a movement animation could use the Ease-In animation curve to add a bit of realism. We'll also learn to change the duration of an animation and to follow one animation with another. The perceived speed of an animation gives subtle cues to our users about what has happened or is about to happen. Subtle clues are the ones that seem to make a deeper impression.

4.1 Animation Timing Curves

CAMediaTimingFunction is the abstract class that defines what a timing function is. It defines four built-in timing functions and allows us to define our own custom timing functions. We will be going over all the options in this section, including how to use them and what effect they have on our animations.

Remember that the time values are normalized. In other words, the time values for the functions are scaled to be between 0 and 1. You can think of normalized time as a percentage of the time the animation will run. All the animation timing curves expect that the time is normalized, so this becomes important to understand as we dive into manipulating the functions.

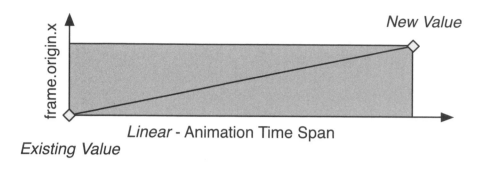

Linear Animation Timing

The linear animation timing function provides straight-line interpolation between the initial point (the fromValue) and the final value (the toValue). The animation curve is shown in Figure 4.1. It has a constant slope from the initial value to the final value (that is what makes it a line, after all).

Recall our discussion of interpolation in Chapter 2, *Cocoa Animation*, on page 9. The animation timing function interpolates the values between the initial and final as described. In the world of animation, this is sometimes referred to as *tweening*, which is short for "in-betweening." This is the process of "filling in" the intermediate frames between two end frames.

Ease-In Animation Timing

Next let's take a look at the Ease-In curve that allows the animation to start slow, get faster and faster through several frames, and finally become constant again but much faster than the basic curve would be.

Notice the flatter part of the curve at the beginning of the animation time span in Figure 4.2, on the next page. During the first part of the animation, the values don't change much, but as time goes on, the values start to change more quickly so that the value ends up with the same new value as in the basic animation, but the arrival path is much different.

Notice also that the slope of the line changes over time. The slope of the curve is basically the "velocity" or "speed" of the value change. The

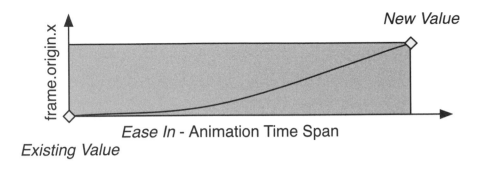

Figure 4.2: EASE-IN ANIMATION INTERPOLATION TIMELINE

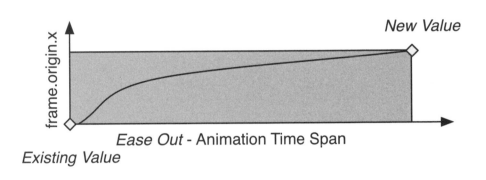

Figure 4.3: EASE-OUT ANIMATION INTERPOLATION TIMELINE

shallower the slope of the curve, the slower the animation appears to change, and conversely, the steeper the curve, the faster the change occurs.

Visually this animation provides a different cue to the user than the basic curve. Since the change starts out slowly, it can give the user time to adjust to the fact that something is changing; then the quick finish provides extra emphasis.

Ease-Out Animation Timing

The Ease-Out timing function provides the opposite effect of the Ease-In function. Instead of starting slow and finishing fast, the Ease-Out timing starts fast and then slows down into its final value. A graph of the values as they change over time is shown in Figure 4.3.

This animation also provides a different cue to the user than the other curves. Since the change starts out quickly, it will draw attention to the initial change. This timing function gives more emphasis to the start of the animation and less to the ending.

Ease-In Ease-Out Animation Timing

The Ease-In Ease-Out timing function starts off slowly, accelerates, and then slows down again to finish slowly. As we can see in Figure 4.4, on the next page, this animation provides a combination of the Ease-In and Ease-Out timing functions.

And as expected, this animation provides a different cue to the user than the other curves. This timing function gives more emphasis to the middle of the animation and less to the beginning and ending.

Custom Animation Timing

The custom timing function allows us to create our own curve using a bezier curve. A bezier curve has two end points and two control points. The end points determine the beginning and end of the curve. The control points define the shape of the curve at the end points (technically a control point defines the tangent to the curve). A curve defined with this method might look like Figure 4.5, on the facing page. It's basically an Ease Middle function since both the beginning and the ending are animating quickly but the middle of the animation is going slowly.

You might have noticed that the values for this curve are also normalized. It helps me to think of this as a percentage of the change in the animation time completed.

We create a custom timing with the initWithControlPoints:::: method on CAMediaTimingFunction like this:

```
- (CAMediaTimingFunction *)getTimingFunction {
        CGFloat c1x = 0.5;
        CGFloat c1y = 1.0;
        CGFloat c2x = 0.5;
        CGFloat c2y = 0.0;
        return [[CAMediaTimingFunction alloc]
                    initWithControlPoints:cx1 :cy1 :cx2 :cy2];
}
```

Since the initial and final values are already known (recall that they are {0, 0} and {1, 1}, respectively), we have to specify only the control points. In our example, we set the first control point to {0.5, 1.0} and the second control point to {0.5, 0.0}. Recall that the control points of

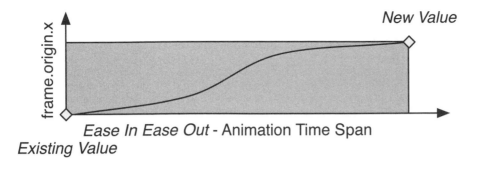

Figure 4.4: EASE-IN EASE-OUT ANIMATION INTERPOLATION TIMELINE

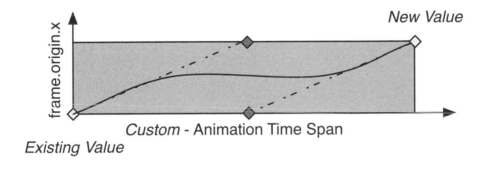

Figure 4.5: CUSTOM ANIMATION INTERPOLATION TIMELINE

a bezier curve define the shape of the curve at that point on the curve (mathematically it's defining the tangent to the curve at that point), so we have set the curve to be sloped up at the beginning and at the end and more or less flat in the middle. This timing function will make the animation change quickly at the beginning and end and change very slowly in the middle. Take a look at the figure again to make sure it makes sense.

Using Ease-In and Ease-Out Animations

The Ease-In and Ease-Out curves work great for giving users subtle clues to what the application is doing. Consider Front Row's display of your song list. As you hold down an arrow key (up or down), the animation gets faster and faster. When you let up on the key, the animation slows gradually. Easing into the very fast animation and easing out of the fast animation instead of an abrupt stop is a great example of using these timing functions to provide subtlety to your users. Another great example of ease-in/out animations is editing the bookmarks for Safari on the iPhone. When you click the Bookmarks button, the list of bookmarks slides in from the bottom with an Ease-Out transition, so it comes on to the screen fast but slows as it gets close to filling the screen. This type of very subtle change in the speed of the animation really gives the app a feeling of "rightness." Things in the real world don't start or stop moving immediately, and making our apps ease in or ease out of animations gives them a real-world feeling.

Timing Function Example

In this example, we will create a custom timing function and use that to time our animation instead of relying on the default linear timing function. Let's dive into the code:

`AnimationTiming/CustomAnimationTiming/MyView.m`

```objc
-(void)setupMover {
  NSRect bounds = self.bounds;
  NSRect moverFrame =
  NSInsetRect(bounds, NSWidth(bounds) / 4.0f,
              NSHeight(bounds) / 4.0f);
  moverFrame.origin.x = 0.0f;
      mover = [[NSImageView alloc] initWithFrame:moverFrame];
      [mover setImageScaling:NSScaleToFit];
      [mover setImage:[NSImage imageNamed:@"photo.jpg"]];
  [self addSubview:mover];
}

- (id)initWithFrame:(NSRect)frame {
  self = [super initWithFrame:frame];
  if (self) {
    [self setupMover];
  }
  return self;
}
```

As we have typically done in other examples, the NIB file contains a single window with an instance of MyView that takes up most of that window. In this code, we are creating and positioning an NSImageView to hold a picture that we are going to animate around our view. We position the picture by simply offsetting the bounds rectangle of our view by one fourth, which centers the mover in the bounds of the view and makes it half as big. We then move it to the left edge by setting the origin.x to zero. Next we process events:

AnimationTiming/CustomAnimationTiming/MyView.m

```
- (BOOL)acceptsFirstResponder {
  return YES;
}

- (void)keyDown:(NSEvent *)event {
  [self move];
}
```

All we do in this code is accept a first responder so we can get key events and then respond to the key events we get by calling move. Next up we see the moving code:

AnimationTiming/CustomAnimationTiming/MyView.m

```
- (CABasicAnimation *)moveAnimation {
  if(nil == moveAnimation) {
    moveAnimation = [CABasicAnimation animation];
    moveAnimation.duration = 2.0f;
    moveAnimation.timingFunction =
    [[CAMediaTimingFunction alloc]
      initWithControlPoints:0.5 :1.0 :0.5 :0.0];
  }
  return moveAnimation;
}

- (void)move {
  NSDictionary *animations = [NSDictionary
                                dictionaryWithObject:[self moveAnimation]
                                forKey:@"frameOrigin"];
  [mover setAnimations:animations];
  NSPoint origin = mover.frame.origin;
  origin.x += NSWidth(mover.frame);
  [mover.animator setFrameOrigin:origin];
}
```

In this code we are creating the animation and then setting its timing function to the custom timing function that we talked about earlier. Recall that this sets a custom curve for the animation interpolation to follow. And remember that we have to set only the control points since the initial and final values are known to be {0, 0} and {1, 1}, respectively. In the move method, we are doing the typical thing of creating an animations dictionary for our mover and adding the custom animation to the dictionary.

In this section, we have seen the curves we can use to control the timing of individual animations. Now let's take a look at using the NSAnimation-Context to control the overall animation duration for a set of animations.

4.2 Cocoa Animation Timing

As discussed previously, animations default to 0.25 seconds to change the property value from the original value to the final value. This makes for a snappy user experience and looks great in most cases. However, from time to time you might want an animation to have a longer or shorter duration. You change the default animation timing by setting the current animation context's duration like this:

```
[NSAnimationContext beginGrouping];
[[NSAnimationContext currentContext] setDuration:2.0f];
// your code here
[NSAnimationContext endGrouping];
```

This is an easy way to set the overall duration of a set of animations. Any animation between the beginGrouping and endGrouping calls will animate for the duration specified. A common use for this is to make the animation run slowly when a modifier key is used (for example, holding down the Shift key could cause the animation to run slowly). For us developers, it's a great way to debug our animations. When they are running slowly, we can sometimes find jumps and other undesirable movements. We don't typically leave this functionality as user accessible. Apple did leave the slowed-down animation for minimization in the Dock, so try it and see; hit the Minimize button on a window while holding down the Shift key.

You can also nest these beginGrouping and endGrouping calls to set the duration of groups of animations separately. In other words, we could have two animations running for one second and another animation run for three seconds. And the whole lot could be grouped so that all three animations start concurrently. We will see an example of this later in Section 4.3, *Chaining Animations*, on page 48.

When we want, we can specify the duration of a particular animation by setting the duration property. Using this property overrides the grouping that we do with NSAnimationContext and should be used only in the cases where we explicitly want the animation to always run at the specified duration. To make this work, we create our own animation and set its duration and then add that animation to the animations dictionary on the object being animated. Except for setting the duration, this is the same process we have been following to use custom instead of default animations in the other examples.

This next example has a controller that will let us customize the animation timing. We will add three buttons to the user interface that will set the animation timing to faster, to slower, and then back to the default.

Hitting the Fast button will cause the animation to be done in 0.1 seconds, hitting the Default button will make the animation run in the default 0.25 seconds, and hitting the Slow button will cause the animation to run in 2.0 seconds. So, let's take a look at the code and see how all this happens.

MyController has three action methods that do the work for us. The first method, makeSlow: on line 1, adds a basic animation to the myView.mover for the frameOrigin key and sets it to a two-second duration. This custom animation is used because of the searching mechanism used by the animator (discussed in Chapter 2, *Cocoa Animation*, on page 9). Recall that first it checks the animations dictionary, and if an animation is found there, it's used. So, once we put this animation into the animations dictionary, the animator will use it whenever the frameOrigin property is changed. This animation will stay in effect until we explicitly remove it.

AnimationTiming/CustomizeAnimation2/MyController.m

```
Line 1    - (IBAction)makeSlow:(id)sender {
    -         CABasicAnimation *frameOriginAnimation = [CABasicAnimation animation];
    -         [frameOriginAnimation setDuration:2.0f];
    -         NSDictionary *animations = [NSDictionary dictionaryWithObjectsAndKeys:
    5                                         frameOriginAnimation, @"frameOrigin", nil];
    -         [myView.mover setAnimations:animations];
    -     }
```

That brings us to the setDefault: method on line 1. This method sets the animations dictionary to nil, which will cause the next call to the animator to use the default animation since the animator won't find anything in the animations dictionary:

AnimationTiming/CustomizeAnimation2/MyController.m

```
Line 1    - (IBAction)makeDefault:(id)sender {
    -         [myView.mover setAnimations:nil];
    -     }
```

And finally, the makeFast: method on line 1 sets the animation duration to 0.1 seconds. In this example, we are replacing the full dictionary out of a drive for simplicity, but you could also set the animations dictionary to a mutable dictionary and then just add and remove animations instead:

AnimationTiming/CustomizeAnimation2/MyController.m

```
Line 1  - (IBAction)makeFast:(id)sender {
          CABasicAnimation *frameOriginAnimation = [CABasicAnimation animation];
          [frameOriginAnimation setDuration:0.1f];
          NSDictionary *animations = [NSDictionary dictionaryWithObjectsAndKeys:
     5                                 frameOriginAnimation, @"frameOrigin",nil];
          [myView.mover setAnimations:animations];
        }
```

The NSAnimationContext duration affects only the animations that do not have their duration explicitly set. So if we were to use a context to slow animations, it would not work for the animations that have had their durations set explicitly as outlined here.

4.3 Chaining Animations

Animations can be made to appear to follow one another. For example, we could have an animated button that slides from Off to On, and when it reaches the On position, another part of the UI reveals a set of controls that are useful when the system is on. When the button reaches the Off position, these controls are hidden again.

One way to accomplish this is to provide a delegate for the first animation and have it initiate when it receives the message that the animation is finished. Animations notify their delegates when the animation is begun and when it ends. When the delegate is told the animation has ended, it also passes along a flag indicating whether the animation ran to completion or whether it was stopped before it could finish. By providing a delegate to the first animation, we can initiate the second animation when the first finishes.

Let's take a look at an example to help all this make sense. In this example, we have two pictures (in NSImageViews again) that we are going to animate. But instead of animating them independently, we are going to chain the animations.

Initially, the beach photo starts on the left of the screen, and then it moves to the center (where the snowman starts). As it arrives, the snowman animates from the center to the right side of the screen. As the beach photo arrives, it therefore appears to be pushing the snowman to the right.

In Figure 4.6, on the next page, we can see the center frame of the animation where the beach photo is just about to finish its animation and the snowman is about to start.

Now let's look at the code needed to make this happen. Let's start with the code that makes the views animate:

AnimationTiming/TimedAnimation/TimedAnimation.m

```
Line 1  - (void)right {
            // photo1 is going to move to where photo2 is
            NSPoint newOrigin = [photo2 frame].origin;
            CABasicAnimation *animation =
     5      [self basicAnimationNamed:@"photo1" duration:1.0f];
            animation.delegate = self;
            [photo1 setAnimations:
             [NSDictionary dictionaryWithObject:animation
                                        forKey:@"frameOrigin"]];
    10      [[photo1 animator] setFrameOrigin:newOrigin];
         }

         - (void) reset {
            [photo1 setAnimations:nil];
    15      [photo2 setAnimations:nil];

            NSPoint newPhoto1Origin = NSMakePoint(0.0f, NSMidY([self frame]) -
                                            (NSHeight([photo1 bounds]) / 2.0f));
            NSPoint newPhoto2Origin =
    20      NSMakePoint(NSMidX([self frame]) - (NSWidth([photo2 bounds]) / 2.0f),
                        NSMidY([self frame]) - (NSHeight([photo2 bounds]) / 2.0f));

            [[photo1 animator] setFrameOrigin:newPhoto1Origin];
            [[photo2 animator] setFrameOrigin:newPhoto2Origin];
    25   }
```

This code is invoked by the event handling (that is, keyDown: as in other examples) and causes the two photos to animate either to the right (via the right method) or back to the beginning (via the reset method). There are a couple of things to notice about the right method. First, we are naming the animation on line 5. That will become important in a moment when we look at the delegate method. Second, we are setting the delegate on line 6. As you recall from earlier discussions, the delegate gets notification when the animation finishes.

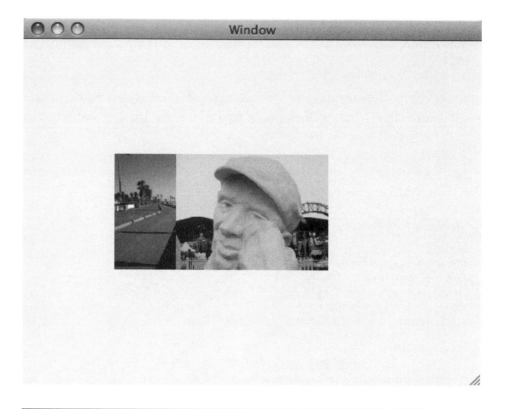

Figure 4.6: CHAINED ANIMATION

AnimationTiming/TimedAnimation/TimedAnimation.m

```
- (void)animationDidStop:(CAAnimation *)animation finished:(BOOL)flag {
    if(flag && [[animation valueForKey:@"name"] isEqual:@"photo1"]) {
        CABasicAnimation *photo2Animation =
        [self basicAnimationNamed:@"photo2" duration:animation.duration];
        [photo2 setAnimations:[NSDictionary dictionaryWithObject:photo2Animation
                                                   forKey:@"frameOrigin"]];
        NSPoint newPhoto2Origin =
        NSMakePoint(NSMaxX([self frame]) - [photo2 frame].size.width,
                    [photo2 frame].origin.y);
        [[photo2 animator] setFrameOrigin:newPhoto2Origin];
    }
}
```

The animationDidStop:finished: method is called when the animation that is attached to photo1 is done. The finished flag will be YES if the animation finished and NO if the animation was stopped prematurely. We want photo2 to move to the left edge when photo1 finishes moving, so we create a new animation with the same duration and add it to photo2 and then tell photo2's animator to move. Something to notice is that the animation for photo2 is not started if the name of the completing animation is not photo1. Using this naming scheme would allow you to use one object as the delegate for more than one animation and then distinguish them using their names.

The view allows us to reset the animation with the R key; therefore, you can reset and run the animation a couple of times to make sure you fully follow what is happening. When the first animation (the attached to photo1) finishes, a second animation (attached to photo2) is created and started. This essentially ties the two animations together.

This example ties two basic animations together, but we can apply this same technique to any of the different animation types. One thing to keep in mind, however, is that the delegate of an animation that is part of an animation group is ignored and not notified when the individual animation is completed. You can, however, attach a delegate to the group and get notification of the group completing.

There's more flexibility in chaining animations when we're using strictly layers in a layer-hosting view. In Chapter 5, *Layer-Backed Views*, on page 53 we will get into putting layers into our views, and in subsequent chapters we will cover a more sophisticated approach to chaining animations.

In this chapter, we have seen how animation timing is configured and used. We can set the duration on our custom animation objects or use the duration of the NSAnimationContext to set the duration. Keep in mind, though, that the animation context provides more flexibility. In the next chapter, we will begin seeing layers in layer-backed views. Adding layers to our tool belt opens up a lot of new and exciting possibilities.

The most exciting phrase to hear in science, the one that heralds new discoveries, is not "Eureka!" but "That's funny...."

▶ Isaac Asimov

Chapter 5

Layer-Backed Views

In this chapter, we are going to see what additional features we gain by making our views layer-backed and start the journey from the Cocoa-oriented animation that we've studied thus far into Core Animation layers. Completing this journey will see us through to the end of the book.

So far, we have been focused on how to use the Core Animation classes that are tightly integrated into Cocoa. Although these approaches provide us with a lot of features and flexibility, we gain even more when we start to use Core Animation layers. You can animate a layer in what is perceived as 3D space. You can also add multiple content types such as QuickTime and OpenGL together in the same layer tree. We will go into each of these areas as we progress through the rest of the book. However, we are not quite ready to dive into full-blown Core Animation layer user interfaces just yet.

Becoming layer-backed is as simple as calling setWantsLayer:. Once a view is layer-backed, three new features are introduced. The first is rotation around the center of the view (we will look at that in Section 5.5, *Rotated Views and Controls*, on page 58). The second is shadows applied to the entire view's content, which will be covered in Section 5.3, *View Shadow*, on page 56. And finally we will cover the third feature, setting the opacity of a view, in Section 5.4, *View Alpha*, on page 58. All of these features have been possible in the past but were much more difficult to code. Thanks to layer backing, it's now a snap to get these effects.

5.1 The Road Ahead

While on this journey, we will be leaving behind some familiar classes and APIs. You will find that Core Animation, while slightly different in some ways, is in many ways very familiar. For example, Core Animation layers are not subclasses of NSResponder, so unlike views, they are unable to process events; however, they do respond to hitTest: to find the layer that was clicked. So, we can still use many of the approaches we are accustomed to in Cocoa. The transition will be gradual and filled with examples to get you up to speed.

This first step along the journey is about backing our views with layers. A layer-backed view has a Core Animation layer as a backing store. Basically, this means any drawing the view does is "cached" into the layer that backs it. Once our drawing is cached in this layer, it is then easy for the system to animate the cached representation in all kinds of interesting ways with blazing-fast performance. In fact, all the animation we have seen thus far in the previous three chapters could have been done with better performance if we'd simply turned on layer backing. Not that we did anything with a taxing performance profile, but if in your experimentation with animation you find delays and other performance problems, then you should try turning on the layer backing and see whether it fixes your problems.

This new flexibility opens up new pitfalls with drawing performance, though. Now, not only do we need to make sure we can draw with acceptable performance (as we have always done), but we also have to make sure that when we draw, we do not adversely affect the animation performance. What this boils down to is that we need to make sure we are following the Cocoa best practices when drawing into our layer-backed views.

Best practice drawing techniques, for example, include drawing only when necessary and drawing only what has actually changed. When appropriate, I'll make sure to point out when to look out for this issue. Before we get into the new features, though, let's take a look at how the layer backing of views works in relation to the view hierarchy that we know so well.

5.2 View and Layer Hierarchy

Let's start with a quick overview of how the layer hierarchy works with layer-backed views. As you know, views in Cocoa are arranged in a tree

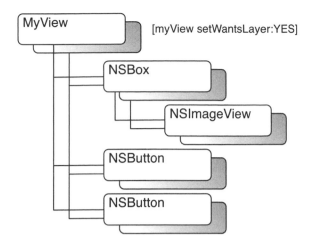

Figure 5.1: VIEW HIERARCHY

starting with the root view and then extending through the subview's array and each of the subview's list of subviews, and so on. In Figure 5.1, we see a set of five views arranged in a typical tree structure. This is referred to as the *view hierarchy*. By default these views would not have a layer, and we would have the typical Cocoa view hierarchy.

When layer backing is switched on via a call to myView.wantsLayer = YES, the view and all its subviews receive layers. In Figure 5.1, we see the layers backing each of the views. This one little line of code opens a lot of new features to us.

Layer-backed views manage their own layers and also manage the layer hierarchy so that the layers stay in sync with the view hierarchy. In other words, if we add a view to the hierarchy, it will get a layer, and that layer will be properly placed in the mirrored layer hierarchy. The same internal management happens when removing views.

Thankfully, most of the time we don't really have to think about our backing layers when coding our applications. The time when this knowledge comes in handy is during debugging when something is not going the way we expect. Knowing the way that the views are managing our layers can sometimes help us find and understand bugs. We also have to be aware of this when we are tracking down and fixing performance issues. So, just keep the hierarchy in mind when you need to find and fix bugs.

Layer Manipulation

Since the view is managing the layer and has to be intimately familiar with what is going on with the layer, it is not recommended that we manipulate the layer in any way except through the methods exposed through the view. As long as we use these methods alone, the view can keep the layer updated and always know what state the layer is in. If we change the layer behind the view, we can end up causing all sorts of interesting and strange drawing and animation behavior. It is possible to have complete control over the layer, but that is the subject of Chapter 8, *Core Animation Layers*, on page 93, where we will be talking about layer-hosting views instead of layer-backed views.

Something else to keep in mind as you integrate layers into your views is that every drawing command we execute results in pushing new data into our layer, which can cause unwanted slowdowns in our animations. We will talk more about this in Section 5.6, *Layer Backing and Performance Concerns*, on page 60.

5.3 View Shadow

Shadows provide a nice way of making a visual element "pop" off the screen. When a view is layer-backed, it can have a shadow attached to it so that it appears to be "higher" than the rest of the content of the window and thus will draw the user's attention.

When we add an NSShadow, the view passes it on to its layer to be rendered when the layer is rendered. The effect is that the drawing done for the view and cached in the layer will have a shadow applied to it. We simply create an instance of NSShadow and configure it the way we'd like and then apply it to our layer-backed view via the setShadow: method.

Figure 5.2: BUTTON WITH SHADOW APPLIED

We can set four properties on a shadow, as described here.

Property Name	Description
opacity	How much the shadow covers the background
radius	How much to blur the shadow's edges
offset	The vertical and horizontal offset of the shadow under the view
color	The color to draw the shadow

Using this technique allows us to get a shadow on all the drawing we do in the view without having to use any low-level Quartz drawing techniques (for the curious, the trick is called *transparency layers*). Since all the drawing is done and then cached in the layer, the system can use the layer as the object to apply the shadow to, and therefore we end up with one shadow for all the drawing instead of a shadow for each part of the drawing. Using this approach makes drawing shadows for our view content much easier.

In Figure 5.2, we see what a button looks like with a shadow applied.

Next is the code that makes that shadow happen. We are simply configuring the shadow with an offset of 10, -10 (positive numbers are to the right and up). The blur radius is set to 10, which is good for this size shadow but looks bad on smaller shadows, so you should play with this setting to get the effect you desire. The color is set to black so that it would be more pronounced in the print copy because the default is dark gray with 33% opacity, which looks great on the screen but washed out in the printed copy.

```
- (void)applyShadow {
    NSShadow *shadow = [[NSShadow alloc] init];
    [shadow setShadowOffset:NSMakeSize(10.0f, -10.0f)];
    [shadow setShadowBlurRadius:10.0f];
    [shadow setShadowColor:[NSColor blackColor]];
    [myButton setShadow:shadow];
}
```

5.4 View Alpha

Alpha (also known as *transparency*) has been available since the first version of Mac OS X, so it has always been possible to draw alpha content into a view. However, as we discussed with shadows, it has never been so easy. In the past, we had to specify the alpha of each component that we drew into a view (each image, each line or circle, and so on). To have a consistent alpha, we had to sometimes convert content (such as JPEGs and such) to get it to have transparency. Using layer-backed mode, however, all we have to do is change the alphaValue property to the desired value, and the whole view and all its drawing will have that alpha value.

5.5 Rotated Views and Controls

Rotated controls are controversial; just take a look at any of the threads on the Cocoa-Dev mailing list to see the varied and passionate opinions about rotating buttons, and you will get a feel for how many different opinions there are about this subject. The Apple user interface "experts" generally argue against the use of rotated controls, claiming that they take away from the consistency of the platform, and generally I agree with them. However, I have seen a few cases where the application genuinely benefited from having a rotated button; typically this has been in scientific applications where the UI just made sense with a rotated button placed along a vertical axis. I say all this to caution you that just because we can rotate controls does not mean we should. They do, however, make it easier to illustrate the points in this section.

Although we have only touched on it previously, since controls (that is, subclasses of NSControl) are views, they can be animated using the same techniques we have been discussing. The really cool part is that these controls continue to work as expected despite being rotated, faded, shadowed, or animated. There are lots of interesting things that can be done once we start applying these techniques to our controls, so let's dive in.

Although it has been possible to rotate a view for a long time (actually since Mac OS X 10.0), most controls have never looked good when rotated and had trouble acting as expected when rotated. For example, buttons would not have the correct activation rectangles and other such undesired behavior. Well, now that we have layer-backed views, we can rotate or otherwise do interesting things with our controls, and they continue to work as expected. In Figure 5.3, on the next page, we see an example of a button that is rotated 45 degrees. Each time the Rotate button is hit, the Beeper button rotates an additional 15 degrees.

Here is the source code that makes the button rotate:

LayerBackedViews/LayerBackedControls/Controller.m

```
Line 1  @implementation Controller

        - (void)awakeFromNib {
            [[rotatingButton superview] setWantsLayer:YES];
     5  }

        - (IBAction) rotateButton:(id)sender {
            CGFloat rotation = [rotatingButton frameCenterRotation];
            [rotatingButton setFrameCenterRotation:
    10          rotation + 15.0f];
        }

        - (IBAction) beep:(id)sender {
            NSBeep();
    15  }
```

As you can see, this code is extremely simple. In the awakeFromNib method on line 3, we make the superview of the button layer-backed (which as you know also makes the button layer-backed as well). Making the superview layer-backed is what makes it possible for the button to still function properly in its rotated state. In the rotateButton: method on line 7, we update the rotation angle.

We can rotate any control or view for that matter by simply turning on layer backing on the view's superview. As we said earlier, it is not recommended that you rotate all the controls in your application simply because you can. Sometimes, though, rotation is the best approach to achieve the effect you want. For example, by rotating a button 90 degrees, you could be highlighting the vertical nature of the button's action. As you work with controls and think through how rotating

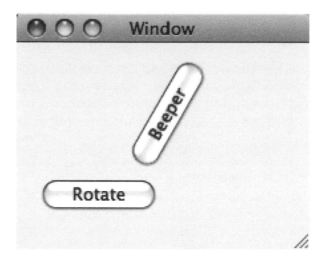

Figure 5.3: UNFILTERED CONTROLS ON BACKGROUND

them might be appropriate, keep in mind (as always) how your users will interpret the rotation, and make sure that it enhances rather than detracts from their experience with your application.

We have to be careful when rotating a view using this technique because if we have changed the anchorPoint of the underlying layer, then we will get undefined behavior. This is one of those cases where we can really cause some unintended drawing and animation if we have manipulated the layer behind the view's back. We will discuss the anchorPoint more later, but when dealing with layer-backed views, it's best not to change this property.

5.6 Layer Backing and Performance Concerns

Once one view in a hierarchy turns on layer backing, each view in that hierarchy has layer backing turned on, regardless of the particular subview's desire. If a subview states that it also wants layer backing, it is redundant. If a subview requests to not be layer-backed, it will be anyway if any of its superview parents (up the view hierarchy) have layer backing turned on. This is important to keep in mind because it can be quite a big memory hog if you are layer-backing views that don't need to be and won't be animating. The important thing to remember is to specify layer backing only on the views that actually need to be layer-

Rotation and User Interface

Another important thing to keep in mind as we rotate user interface elements (controls or other elements of our own making) is the changing validity of the metaphor we are working toward. Using a control in one situation and then simply rotating it without changing its appearance might totally break our metaphor. For example, consider the Dock changes that were part of Leopard. Initially in Leopard your Dock was 3D and reflective as if your application icons were sitting on a shiny shelf. The Dock looked great when it was on the bottom of the screen. However, when the Dock was moved to the right or left side of the screen, it totally broke the metaphor. Shelves do not typically hold content when they are vertical. So, simply rotating the control (the Dock) did not work for the metaphor; it broke in the rotation. Apple responded by making the Dock less 3D when rotated to either side of the screen. This is an important lesson for us to keep in mind as we build our user interfaces.

backed instead of just specifying that the content view of a window is layer-backed.

For example, if we were to turn on layer backing for MyView in Figure 5.4, on the following page, we would get a layer for every view in this hierarchy. The hierarchy is shown in Figure 5.4, on the next page. Notice that despite us requesting that the box not have a layer since its superview is layer-backed, the box will be layer-backed.

In addition, if we were to request layer backing on the box, then the image view and the box would be layer-backed, but the rest of the views would not have a layer. This gives us control over which views actually get layer backing and thus over how much memory we consume with our application. This becomes especially important in view hierarchies that are very deep. If we have twenty-five views that do not animate and five that do, it would be wasteful of memory to have all thirty of the views be layer-backed. Keep in mind that the other twenty-five views can animate their properties through their animator proxy as usual even without a layer backing. The only time we need to turn on layer backing is if we want alpha, center rotation, filters, or a shadow on our view.

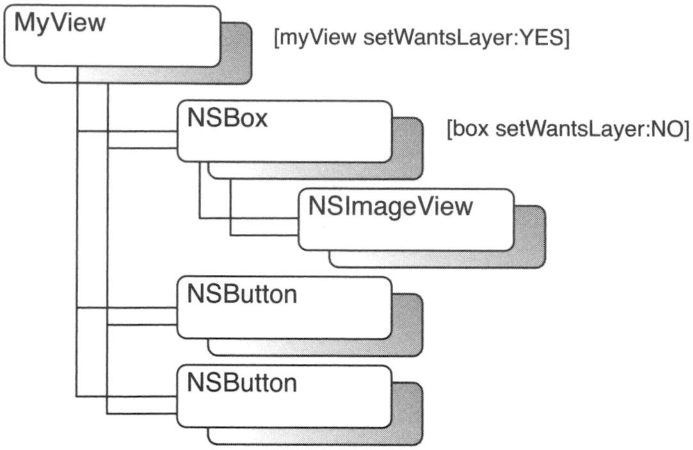

MyView — [myView setWantsLayer:YES]

NSBox — [box setWantsLayer:NO]

NSImageView

NSButton

NSButton

Figure 5.4: VIEW AND LAYER HIERARCHY

Another place where unexpected performance issues can pop up is putting multiple layer trees into a single window. Each independent layer tree requires its own rendering context, which can consume a lot of resources. So if you have multiple sections in your UI that would naturally fit into multiple views, try to make the UI with a single root layer and then have the multiple sections of your UI be sublayers of that one root.

We have seen the final Cocoa-like features of animation in this chapter. In the next chapter, we will get further into the Core Animation with the addition of filters to our views. And in the chapter after that, we will be fully engaged with Core Animation and layer-based APIs.

*If I were to wish for anything, I should not wish for wealth
and power, but for the passionate sense of potential—for
the eye which, ever young and ardent, sees the possible.
Pleasure disappoints; possibility never.*

► Søren Kierkegaard

Chapter 6

Filtered Views

In Mac OS X Leopard we have more than 125 different filters to correct
the color, sharpen, distort, and stylize. We can preview the full set with
the CI Filter Browser widget (in a typical install, you can find the widget
at /Developer/Extras/Core Image/CI Filter Browser.wdgt). And we can use and
combine all these filters to modify the look of our layer-backed views.

Core Image filters let us use the GPU to manipulate images. Besides
the blindingly fast performance that we get from using the GPU to do
the image manipulation, Core Image also allows us to use the sophisticated OpenGL shading language to write our own custom filters. An
exploration of Core Image could fill a book all its own. In this chapter,
we focus on how filters apply to Core Animation.

Recall that a layer-backed view has its drawing content cached in its
layer. Once the content of the view is cached, you can then treat it much
like you would an image. In fact, that is how the filtering works with
views. Once you turn on layer backing and once the view's drawing is
cached, you can apply Core Image filters, and they act on the cached
drawing just as they would an image. There are countless ways you can
use these filters, and as you gain more experience, your imagination
will run wild with what is possible.

Another really cool thing you can do with these filters is to use the
transition filters for transitioning between subviews. We will learn how
to use the CI transition filters in this chapter.

One commonly used Core Image filter is Bloom. A Bloom filter softens
the edges of an image and brightens the lighter parts. Overall, it makes
the image appear softer and as if it were glowing. We can adjust and
animate a couple of properties in the Bloom filter. The first is the radius.
The radius specifies how many pixels are used in the effect (the larger
the radius, the greater the effect of the filter). The second attribute is the

intensity of the filter. A common use of this filter is to highlight a layer. And if the intensity of the filter is animated, then the content of the layer will appear to pulse. This is really cool and can be used to great effect with UI elements. One in particular from Apple's World Wide Developer Conference (WWDC) demos of Core Animation is a recipe application's menu system. As the user changes the selected recipe, a pulsing white rectangle follows the selection.

The examples that I develop in this chapter are more focused on how the technologies fit together. I purposefully chose to use filters that are less commonly used than something like Bloom. I want you to see how things work without having to think about things like "Oh, that would be prettier if it had a shadow." I use filters that are unlikely to be used in a real application so that you can focus on how to apply the filters. I will leave the beautification of your application with the perfect filter effects to you.

Let's get started with a quick overview of what the filters are and how we use them.

6.1 View Filters

You can apply filters in three different ways to layer-backed views: backgroundFilters, contentFilters, and compositingFilters. As the names imply, the filters act on different parts of the view.

The background filters will apply the filter to the background of the view. The background is any part of the view that is not drawn on. Another way to think about it is that any part of the view's superview that is visible through the view will have the filtered applied. A background filter might be used to emphasize a view by softly blurring the background (via one of the blur filters).

Filters in the contentFilters array are applied to the view but not to the background. Any drawing done in the view will have the content filter applied. Using a content filter is a good way to change the user's perception of the content to either emphasize it or de-emphasize it.

Finally, compositingFilters allow us to change the way our view content is composited with the background content. There is a huge range of compositing operations possible from simply replacing the background (the default) to inverting the colors of the background.

The filters are chained together for us and applied in order from the first to the last filter. Each filter's inputImage is set to the outputImage of the previous filter. The first filter's inputImage will be the content of the view as cached in the layer, and the outputImage of the last filter is what will be displayed. This chaining behavior takes care of the input and output images of all the filters, so you don't have to set any of these keys for the filters.

Once a filter is attached to a layer-backed view, the layer becomes a "manager" of sorts for the filter. Don't manipulate the filter directly once it is attached to a view. Instead, use key-value coding (KVC) to modify the filter. For example, if you have a Box Blur filter attached as a content filter of a view, don't change the radius directly. Use the KVC method called setValue:forKeyPath: on the view like this:

```
[myView setValue:[NSNumber numberWithFloat:2.5]
       forKeyPath:@"contentFilters.myFilter.inputRadius"]
```

This way, the view knows when the filter is changed so that it can take the appropriate action (apply the changed filter, cache the result, and so on). If you make changes to the filter without going through the layer, you will have some undefined behavior. From experience, typically the filter stops being applied, but occasionally garbage is copied to the screen.

Another thing that is often confusing with filters that are attached to a view or layer is that they should be given a unique name. Despite that the various filters types (background, content, and composite) are stored in arrays, the view or layer finds the filters as if they were in a dictionary. For example, in the code before the key path, contentFilters.myFilter.inputRadius looks in the array of contentFilters for a filter named myFilter. Once found, it sets the value for the key inputRadius. Now for the part that confuses people: the CIFilter class method filterWithName: expects the name of the filter class (that is, CIBoxFilter), not the name of the instance. So once you create the filter (with filterWithName:), you need to set the new instance's name. The code will look something like this to create an instance of the CIPointillize filter:

```
CIFilter *pointalize = [CIFilter filterWithName:@"CIPointillize"
                              keysAndValues:kCIInputRadiusKey,
                                            [NSNumber numberWithFloat:1.0f],
                                            kCIInputCenterKey, center, nil];
pointalize.name = @"pointalize";
// later in the code we would have this line of code to change
// the value of the inputRadius for the filter
[myView setValue:[NSNumber numberWithFloat:14.0f]
              forKeyPath:[NSString stringWithFormat:
                  @"contentFilters.pointalize.%@", kCIInputRadiusKey]];
```

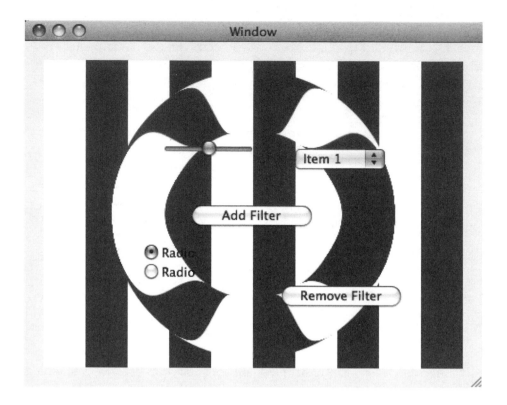

Figure 6.1: BACKGROUND FILTER APPLIED

The important thing to remember here is that you need to set the name property on the filter to be able to change its values once it's added to one of the filter arrays on your view.

6.2 Background Filters

As you know, views have drawing done in them only by the view's own drawRect: or by any of the view's subviews that implement drawRect:. The rest of the view's bounds are left as transparent, and the superview will "show through" the view. This transparent area is the "background" to which the filters are applied. Let's look at an example to get a feel for what applying a background filter looks like.

In Figure 6.1, the background view draws blue stripes so that the filter can be better seen. The view in the foreground has a bunch of controls as subviews. The view containing the controls has a CITorusLensDistortion filter applied (and its width is animated), which is essentially like placing a glass distortion in the shape of a torus over the background. Notice that the background filter is applied only to the superview. None of the controls is filtered. In fact, the controls continue to function as usual, without regard to the filter. Let's look at the code to see how this all works:

FilteredViews/BackgroundFilteredView/BackgroundFilteredView.m

```
Line 1  - (void) applyFilter {
            CIVector *center = [CIVector
                                vectorWithX:NSMidX([self bounds])
                                Y:NSMidY([self bounds])];
     5      CIFilter *torus = [CIFilter filterWithName:@"CITorusLensDistortion"
                                    keysAndValues:kCIInputCenterKey, center,
                                kCIInputRadiusKey, [NSNumber numberWithFloat:150.0f],
                                kCIInputWidthKey, [NSNumber numberWithFloat:2.0f],
                                kCIInputRefractionKey, [NSNumber numberWithFloat:1.7f],
    10                          nil];
            torus.name = @"torus";

            [controls setBackgroundFilters:[NSArray arrayWithObjects:torus, nil]];
            [self addAnimationToTorusFilter];
    15  }
```

The applyFilter method on line 1 is responsible for creating the filter and adding it to the backgroundFilters property of the controls subview as well as attaching the animation. Using the filter, as you can see, is very simple; most of the code in this method is just setting up the torus filter:

FilteredViews/BackgroundFilteredView/BackgroundFilteredView.m

```
Line 1  - (void) addAnimationToTorusFilter {
            NSString *keyPath = [NSString stringWithFormat:
                                @"backgroundFilters.torus.%@",
                                kCIInputWidthKey];
     5      CABasicAnimation *animation = [CABasicAnimation
                                        animationWithKeyPath:keyPath];
            animation.fromValue = [NSNumber numberWithFloat:50.0f];
            animation.toValue = [NSNumber numberWithFloat:80.0f];
            animation.duration = 1.0;
    10      animation.repeatCount = 1e100f;
            animation.timingFunction = [CAMediaTimingFunction functionWithName:
                                        kCAMediaTimingFunctionEaseInEaseOut];
            animation.autoreverses = YES;
            [[controls layer] addAnimation:animation forKey:@"torusAnimation"];
    15  }
```

Adding the animation is similarly simple; all you have to do is create the animation, configure it, and then add it to the layer of your view. Here are some things to note about how this animation is applied: with the keyPath, notice that it's set to backgroundFilters.torus.kCIInputWidth. back-groundFilters is the key into the filters list of our view. torus is the name you gave to the filter in applyFilter. And the kCIInputWidthKey is a constant that specifies the width property of the torus filter.

The really cool part is that all the properties of the filter can be simi-larly animated. If you wanted to animate the outer radius of the torus from 120 to 180, you'd simply create a new animation that was tied to backgroundFilters.torus.kCIInputRadiusKey and set its toValue to 120 and its fromValue to 180. Adding this animation to the layer would then cause the outer radius of the torus to animate in addition to the width. Then you'd have two animations going on at once. You can even add several filters and animate each of them independently. Of course, you can go overboard too and overwhelm your users. Moderation is the best course of action. There are so many cool things to do that it's hard not to get carried away!

FilteredViews/BackgroundFilteredView/BackgroundFilteredView.m

```
Line 1    - (void)awakeFromNib {
             [self setWantsLayer:YES];
             [self applyFilter];
          }
```

The awakeFromNib method on line 1 is adding the filter when the NIB file is loaded, but more important, it is setting the view to be layer-backed. For the background filters to be applied, the superview must be layer-backed (which will in turn make the view layer-backed as well).

6.3 Content Filters

A content filter lets you filter the content of the view instead of the background. We'll explore this idea by manipulating controls as you would any other view content. If you apply a filter to the content of a view, all the content including controls will have that filter applied to it. I'm not suggesting that you apply filters to controls as a typical use case, but it does serve our purpose here of seeing what applying these filters can do for us.

Let's take a look at an example to help solidify our knowledge of filters on the content of layer-backed views. This example has two views: the background view that is responsible for drawing the stripes and putting the content filter onto its only subview and the subview that does noth-ing but hold a set of controls. The UI is shown in Figure 6.2, on the next page.

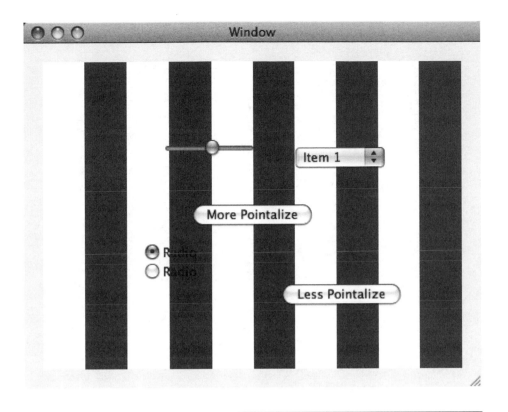

Figure 6.2: SIMPLE FILTERS EXAMPLE USER INTERFACE

If you click the Heavy Pointalize button, you will see the filter applied to the content of the controls view. The effect is shown in Figure 6.3, on the following page. The Pointalize filter pixilates its input image into round pixels (instead of square). You are setting the radius of these points by hitting the Heavy Pointalize or Light Pointalize button.

Notice that this time the background is unchanged, and only the content is altered. If you have the application running, spend a couple of seconds observing the change between the heavy and light pointalized filters to get a feel for what is changing. We will look at the code shortly, but let's take a look at the rest of the interface for just a moment.

Pointalize is probably not a filter you would apply very often to a set of controls, but it helps make the point that even though the filter might render your UI unreadable, it does not render the controls ineffective. You can still click the buttons (heavy and light) and also use pop-ups. As you can see in Figure 6.4, on page 71, when you click the pop-up,

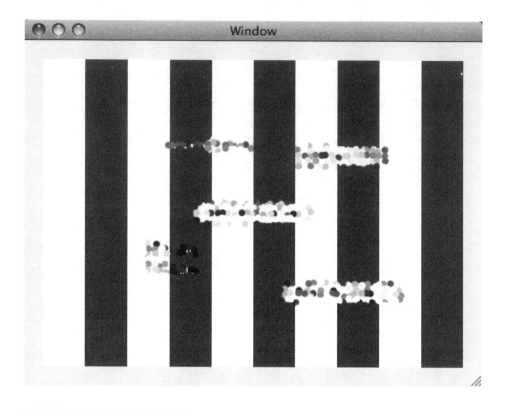

Figure 6.3: Pointalized user interface

the menu does not have the filter applied. That is because the menu is not part of the view hierarchy of the controls view.

Now that you've seen the UI, let's dig into the code and see how all this fits together. As always, applying these filters requires the views to be layer-backed, so the view is set to wanting a layer with the setWantsLayer: in awakeFromNib. You could have set the flag in IB, but I like to have the line of code so that it's explicit. As you get comfortable with this stuff, feel free to flip the switch in IB instead of continuing to code it.

FilteredViews/FilteredView/FilteredView.m

```
- (void)awakeFromNib {
  [controls setWantsLayer:YES];
}
```

Next up you pointalize the view by applying the CIPointillize filter. Again, as in our previous example, most of the code in this method is just

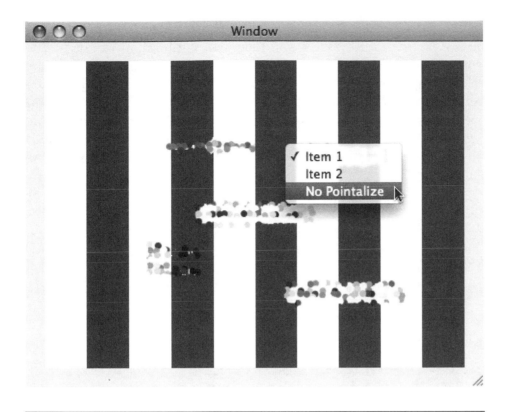

Figure 6.4: POP-UP IN A POINTALIZED USER INTERFACE

configuring the filter. Actually applying it to our view is only one line of code. You named the filter here just as you did earlier even though you are not animating it. You will still need the filter's name later as you modify it through the setValue:forKeyPath: method.

`FilteredViews/FilteredView/FilteredView.m`

```
Line 1   - (void)pointalze {
             CIVector *center = [CIVector vectorWithX:NSMidX([self bounds])
                                                     Y:NSMidY([self bounds])];
             CIFilter *pointalize = [CIFilter
    5                             filterWithName:@"CIPointillize"
                                  keysAndValues:kCIInputRadiusKey,
                                  [NSNumber numberWithFloat:1.0f],
                                  kCIInputCenterKey, center, nil];
             pointalize.name = @"pointalize";
    10       [controls setContentFilters:[NSArray arrayWithObjects:pointalize, nil]];
         }
```

On line 7 in the heavyPointalize: method, you are creating the Pointalize filter if it's not already there and then setting the input radius to 5.0f. Notice that we are going through the key-value coding method to set the value as we discussed earlier. If you ever get very strange, unexpected behavior from your filters, take a look at the code to make sure you are modifying the filters through the KVC methods like you are doing here. The lightPointalize method is doing basically the same thing but setting the radius to 1.0 instead. And finally, noPointalize removes the filter altogether.

FilteredViews/FilteredView/FilteredView.m

```
Line 1   - (IBAction)noPointalize:(id)sender {
             if(0 < [[controls contentFilters] count]) {
               [controls setContentFilters:nil];
             }
      5  }

         - (IBAction)heavyPointalize:(id)sender {
             if(nil == [controls contentFilters] ||
                 0 == [[controls contentFilters] count]) {
     10      [self pointalze];
             }
             NSString *path = [NSString stringWithFormat:
                               @"contentFilters.pointalize.%@", kCIInputRadiusKey];
             [controls setValue:[NSNumber numberWithInt:5.0f] forKeyPath:path];
     15  }

         - (IBAction)lightPointalize:(id)sender {
             if(nil == [controls contentFilters] ||
                 0 == [[controls contentFilters] count]) {
     20      [self pointalze];
             }
             NSString *path = [NSString stringWithFormat:
                               @"contentFilters.pointalize.%@", kCIInputRadiusKey];
             [controls setValue:[NSNumber numberWithInt:1.0f]
     25          forKeyPath:path];
         }
```

You will probably never want to apply the Pointalize filter to controls in a real application, however. The point of this example is to show you what is possible with the filters in a way that shows up well when printed. In a real application, you would apply filters to your user interface elements to focus the user's attention. Next up we will take a look at compositing your view content into its background and see how the compositing filters work.

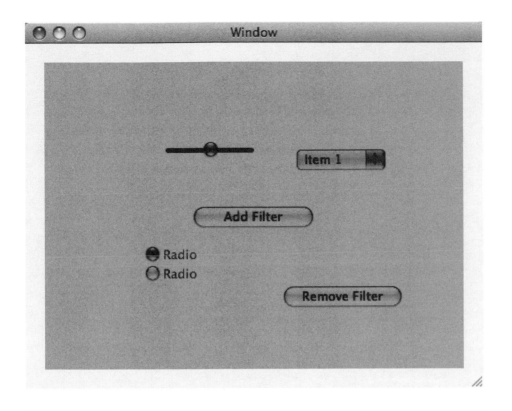

Figure 6.5: COLOR BURN CONTROLS INTO BACKGROUND

6.4 Compositing Filters

Compositing filters take the view's content and combine or mix it with the content of the superview. The default composite type (although it's not necessarily implemented as a composite operation) is Source Over, which means the foreground image is mixed with the background image based on its opacity. The more transparent, the more the background image shows through. We can choose from almost two dozen composite operations. Each has a slightly different approach to mixing the two images. Once you've introduced the basics using Color Burn Blend Mode, play with the other options to get a feel for what is possible.

Color Burn Blend Mode takes the foreground colors and uses them to darken the background. Let's take a look at the UI with this composite filter applied. In Figure 6.5, we see the controls "burned" into the background.

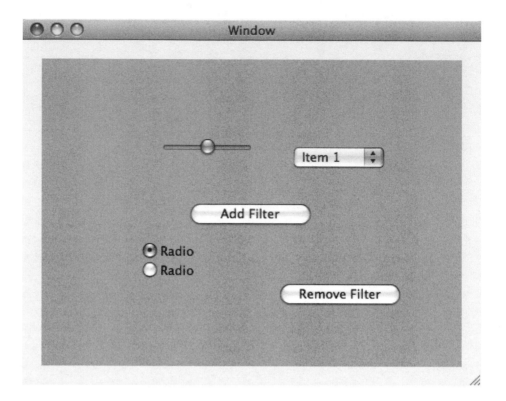

Figure 6.6: UNFILTERED CONTROLS ON BACKGROUND

In this UI, the background view simply fills its frame with a light gray color, and the controls view (that has all the buttons and so on in it) is composited into the background view with the Color Burn Blend Mode filter. The filter darkens all the controls and makes the whole UI look darker. Recall, though, that all these controls are still active and can be used just as any other control would be used. In this example, the Remove Filter button is hooked up to remove the filter from the control's view. Try clicking it, and see the UI change to look like Figure 6.6.

Let's take a quick look at the code to make compositing filters happen:

FilteredViews/CompositedView/CompositedView.m

```
Line 1   @implementation CompositedView

    -    - (void) applyFilter {
    -        CIFilter *filter = [CIFilter filterWithName:@"CIColorBurnBlendMode"
    5                                 keysAndValues:nil];
    -        [[controls animator] setCompositingFilter:filter];
    -    }
    -
```

```
   - (void) removeFilter {
10   [[controls animator] setCompositingFilter:nil];
   }

   - (void)awakeFromNib {
     [self setWantsLayer:YES];
15   [self applyFilter];
   }

   - (IBAction)removeFilter:(id)sender {
     if(nil != [controls compositingFilter]) {
20     [self removeFilter];
     }
   }

   - (IBAction)addFilter:(id)sender {
25   if(nil == [controls compositingFilter]) {
       [self applyFilter];
     }
   }

30   - (void)drawRect:(NSRect)rect {
     [[NSColor lightGrayColor] set];
     NSRectFill(rect);
   }

35 @end
```

Notice on line 3 in method applyFilter that the addition and configuration of the filter is very simple. You don't need to set the background or foreground images; they will be set automatically for you by the view. You can combine these effects in any way you want. Something to keep in mind, however, when using filters in your user interface is that the effects (especially when applied to controls) can be a distraction to the user, so make sure that any effect you apply leads the user to understanding better what is going on with the application.

So, we have run the course of digging into Cocoa-based Core Animation techniques. We have seen a lot of fantastic techniques on how to add animations to your user interfaces, but we are about to depart into a whole new world of three-dimensional animation that is possible with the use of pure Core Animation layers.

The great thing is that all we've learned will transfer directly to the discussion of layers. How do we make more than one animation happen at the same time? We use CAAnimationGroup, the same class we used to group animations on views. The timing, filters, and other functionality all transfer directly into our use of layers. It's going to be fun, so let's get started.

If we all worked on the assumption that what is accepted as true were really true, there would be little hope of advance.

► Orville Wright

Chapter 7

Core Animation

At its heart, Core Animation is based on a concept called a *layer* (in fact, its code name was Layer Kit). A layer is basically a two-dimensional surface that can be animated in three dimensions. Being two-dimensional, layers do not have depth, but since they can be placed and animated in a 3D space, they can be placed at various depth locations in a scene.

This is the trick to the look of applications such as Front Row or UI elements such as Cover Flow in iTunes or the Finder. The icons that move around on the platter in Front Row as you change a selection in the initial screen are two-dimensional images placed on a 3D platter and then moved along the outer rim of that platter as you change a selection. Cover art in iTunes is arranged with a perspective transformation so that the unselected album art looks like it's placed behind the selected cover art and rotated slightly. These treatments (and many more) are possible only when using Core Animation's layers.

Another feature that is present only in layers is mixing media types in the same view. For example, if your application uses Quartz Composer compositions and QuickTime media and you want to have both types of media playing at the same time in the same view, you will have to use a set of Core Animation layers to accomplish that. We will start this chapter with an example that mixes content types so you can see just how easy it is with Core Animation.

In this and the next couple of chapters, we are going to build a Front Row–like application as a vehicle to learn the Core Animation APIs. We will start with the menu in this chapter, and in subsequent chapters we will build out the rotating platter of icons and a menu that looks a lot like the menu for Front Row. Let's get started with layer-hosting views.

7.1 Layer-Hosting Views

Layer-backed views are conceptually similar to the regular Cocoa view programming model. The difference is that the backing store for the view is a layer. Apart from giving us a lot of additional capabilities, there really is no difference in the way we deal with views that are layer-backed and those that are not layer-backed. In other words, we have many new capabilities with few new concepts to learn. When a view is layer backed, the view controls and owns the layer. When a view merely hosts layers, we own and manage them instead. That gives us a lot more flexibility. In this section, we will see how to make our views host our layer-based creations.

We need to keep a couple of things in mind when writing views to host layers. First, the view that hosts a layer should not do any drawing of its own. The drawing is typically ignored, and if it is done, it is typically drawn over by the layer anyway. Instead, do any custom drawing within a layer (we will talk about that later). Second, the view is going to be responsible for all the event handling for the layers that it hosts. Layers are not NSResponders, so they don't have the mechanisms to respond to events. Instead, our view will have to handle all the events and invoke whatever code is required from the user's actions. We can place subviews into a layer-hosting view, however, which can sometimes make handling the events easier.

Unlike views, layers are able to host several different kinds of content. We can put Quartz Composer content in one layer and an OpenGL drawing in another layer and have them both be part of the same superlayer. And since layers are able to do this, we are able to freely combine content into our user interfaces. The following example shows a little of what is possible with layer-hosting views.

In Figure 7.1, on the facing page, we can see a Quartz Composer composition running in the background of our view, along with an NSImageView placed over the composition. The image view has its opacity set to 75% so that we can see the composition through it (of course, you don't get much animation on paper, so run the example as soon as you can to get the real feel).

Before layers, this was very difficult indeed. We would have had to create a transparent window to host the NSImageView and then make sure that window tracked with the underlying window. Overall, it's a huge amount of complex code. Now we can do this with about three or four lines of code.

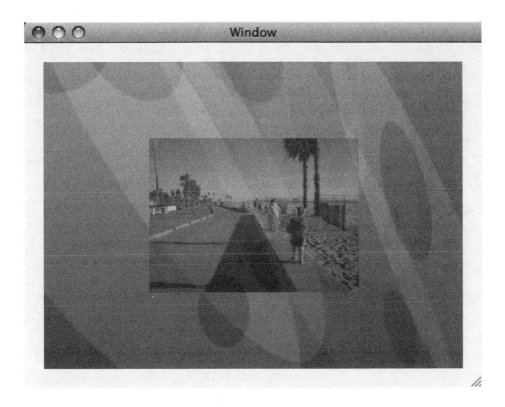

Figure 7.1: QUARTZ COMPOSER BACKGROUND

Let's look at the code now to see how it all works:

CoreAnimation/QCBackground/SharedContentView.m

```
Line 1    - (CALayer *)makeCompositionLayer {
              QCCompositionRepository *repo =
              [QCCompositionRepository sharedCompositionRepository];
              QCComposition *composition =
    5         [repo compositionWithIdentifier:@"/moving shapes"];
              QCCompositionLayer *compLayer =
              [QCCompositionLayer compositionLayerWithComposition:composition];
              CGColorRef cgcolor = CGColorCreateGenericRGB(0.25f, 0.675, 0.1, 1.0);
              [compLayer setValue:(id)cgcolor
    10                 forKeyPath:[NSString stringWithFormat:@"patch.%@.value",
                                   QCCompositionInputPrimaryColorKey]];
              [compLayer setValue:[NSNumber numberWithFloat:5.0f]
                         forKeyPath:[NSString stringWithFormat:@"patch.%@.value",
                                   QCCompositionInputPaceKey]];
    15        CGColorRelease(cgcolor);
              return compLayer;
          }
```

We create the layer on line 6 in the makeCompositionLayer method. As you can see, most of the code here deals with getting the composition from the composition repository and configuring the composition. Once we have the composition, creating the layer is only one line of code. Notice that we created a specific subclass of CALayer to host the composition, namely, the QCCompositionLayer. This type is specifically geared toward Quartz Composer compositions and handles all the complexity of running the composition for us. There are other layer types focused on OpenGL and QuickTime content, so use those when appropriate.

I hope this small example has piqued your interest in using layers and the possibilities they present for making very interesting user interfaces. In the rest of this chapter, we are going to study the details of how to build CALayer-based user interfaces.

7.2 Forming UIs with Layers

In Cocoa, user interfaces are built by composing views into a hierarchy that presents a set of controls such as buttons and sliders as well as custom views that we write ourselves. Together these views make up the user interface and are able to process events and respond to user actions by redrawing or invoking an application action. Core Animation builds on this familiar paradigm of organizing the elements in a tree. Layers have *sublayers* and a *superlayer* that mirror their NSView counterparts of subviews and the superview. So if you are already familiar with the view hierarchy, you will have no trouble picking up the layer hierarchy.

In addition to the layer tree, we will also be covering the style properties of layers. Layers have many different properties that give us extensive control over the style and look of the layer. For example, a layer can have a border and rounded corners. Each of these properties can be animated, and we will look at them in detail later in this section.

We will also cover the coordinate system of layers in detail. A few things might work differently than you would expect, so we will cover these concepts in detail. We will also talk about how the layers fit into their 3D world and how to manipulate them in 3D space. Let's dive into the layer tree to get our first look at how layers work.

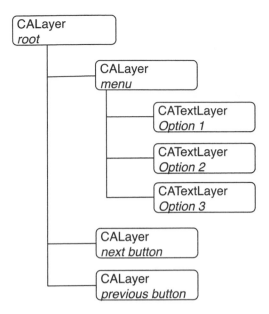

Figure 7.2: EXAMPLE LAYER TREE

7.3 Organizing Layers in Trees

Each layer can have one superlayer and as many sublayers as needed. We refer to this as a *tree* because there is a *root* layer (the layer without a superlayer) and sublayers that extend out like branches until finally we reach a layer with no sublayers (sometimes referred to as *leaves* in the tree). In Figure 7.2, we see what a layer tree might look like for the menu in an application such as Front Row.

The root layer is at the top left (labeled *root*) and has three sublayers (menu, next button, and previous button). The menu layer also has three sublayers (Option 1, Option 2, and Option 3). Here is the code needed to make this layer tree:

`CoreAnimation/SimpleMenu/MyController.m`

```
Line 1   - (void)awakeFromNib {
             CALayer *layer = [CALayer layer];
             layer.backgroundColor = [self black];
             [view setLayer:layer];
      5      [view setWantsLayer:YES];
             [view.layer addSublayer:[self menuLayer]];
         }
```

In the awakeFromNib method on line 1, the initial root layer is configured to have a black background. We can't just use an NSColor here instead of calling out to a custom method because layers rely on the data types of Quartz instead of their AppKit counterparts. We will look at the code to create the Quartz colors briefly in a moment.

After configuring the layer, we add it to the view. Notice the order here: we first provide a layer to the view, and then we tell the view it wants a layer. If we did things in the opposite order, the view would be creating a layer for itself that is discarded in the next method call, so it's best to call these two methods in this order. By providing the layer for the view, we have made it a layer-hosting view. Typically the view will do no drawing and will instead respond only to events. In fact, in this case we are not even using a custom view yet. The view is just an instance of NSView. Later as we develop this example, we will switch to a custom subclass that will process our events.

And finally, after setting up the root layer, we add the menu layer. We do not size or do any other layout on the root layer. The view will take care of the positioning and sizing of the root layer for us. The rest of the layers are up to us to lay out. It's important to remember this as you build your layer-based UI. Often developers forget that only the root layer is automatically laid out. As a result, sublayers are not drawn or don't show up where they are expected. We will look at the layout in detail later in this chapter.

CoreAnimation/SimpleMenu/MyController.m

```
Line 1   - (CALayer *)menuLayer {
    -        CGFloat offset = 10.0f;
    -        CALayer *menu = [CALayer layer];
    -        menu.name = @"menu";
    5        NSRect bounds = [view bounds];
    -        NSRect rect = NSInsetRect(bounds, bounds.size.width / 4.0f, offset);
    -        rect.origin.x += bounds.size.width / 4.0f - offset;
    -        menu.frame = NSRectToCGRect(rect);
    -        menu.borderWidth = 2.0f;
    10       menu.borderColor = [self white];
    -        NSArray *names = [NSArray arrayWithObjects:
    -                            @"Option 1", @"Option 2", @"Option 3", nil];
    -        NSArray *items = [self menuItemsFromNames:names
    -                                          offset:offset
    15                                            size:menu.frame.size];
    -        [menu setSublayers:items];
    -        return menu;
    -    }
```

Text Layers and Strings

We can do a lot more with CATextLayer than this simple example shows. Instead of using a straight NSString and therefore having a single font and color, we could instead use an NSAttributed-String, and then we could use much of the expressive power of the attributed string. As we said in the main text, the CATextLayer is not a full-fledged layout engine, but it is capable of doing a lot more than simply displaying a string in a single font and color. If you have more advanced text requirements for your application, make sure to look into the attributed string and see whether it will do what you need before resorting to the drawing techniques that are discussed later in this chapter.

Another aspect of the text layer that this example does not bring out is truncation of the string. Since we know the length of our menu item strings will fit in the menu layer, we don't have to worry about it. But if you do in your app, you can set the truncationMode property on the text layer to kCATruncationStart, kCATruncationEnd, or kCATruncationMiddle to get the layer to truncate the string for us according to the size we set.

The menuLayer method on line 1 creates and configures the layer used for the menu. First up we initialize the offset to use between layers and at the top and side of the parent layer (in other words, the distance between the edge of the menu layer and the first option in the menu and the distance between the other options). Next we create the menu and name it. Naming the layers is not necessary, but it helps when debugging and during layout, so I typically name my layers.

Next we calculate a frame for the menu. The menu layer should take up the right half of the parent layer and be offset from the top and bottom. The NSInsetRect function takes care of the math for us. Basically, it shrinks the rectangle by twice the arguments passed in as the width and height (the first and second arguments) and then moves the origin of the rectangle. The net effect is that the center of the rectangle remains in the same spot and the rest of it shrinks. Next we move the layer over to the right edge of the root layer and finally set the frame. Doing the layout manually is a bit tedious, but there is often no other way to get the exact effect you want, so it's important that we go into it. There are easier ways to do the layout if you don't need exact control. We will go over layout managers shortly.

Next we set the border color and width. Although this is often not necessary in a real user interface, it is very useful for debugging. With the border set, you can see exactly where the layer is. This is a technique that web developers use quite often to find layout bugs.

CoreAnimation/SimpleMenu/MyController.m

```
Line 1   - (NSArray *)menuItemsFromNames:(NSArray *)itemNames
                                offset:(CGFloat)offset
                                  size:(CGSize)size {
           NSMutableArray *menuItems = [NSMutableArray array];
     5     CGFloat fontSize = 24.0f;
           NSFont *font = [NSFont boldSystemFontOfSize:fontSize];
           int counter = 1;
           for(NSString *itemName in itemNames) {
             CATextLayer *layer = [CATextLayer layer];
    10       layer.string = itemName;
             layer.name = itemName;
             layer.foregroundColor = [self white];
             layer.font = font;
             layer.fontSize = fontSize;
    15       layer.alignmentMode = kCAAlignmentCenter;
             CGSize preferredSize = [layer preferredFrameSize];
             CGFloat width = (size.width - preferredSize.width) / 2.0f;
             CGFloat height = size.height -
             counter * (offset + preferredSize.height);
    20       layer.frame = CGRectMake(width, height,
                                 preferredSize.width, preferredSize.height);
             [menuItems addObject:layer];
             counter++;
           }
    25     return menuItems;
         }
```

Then we create the menu items and add them as sublayers. Let's look at how the items are created starting on line 6. We first grab the bold system font at size 24 so the menu gets an easy-to-read font. Then we iterate through the names and make a new layer for each name. In this step, we are using a subclass of CALayer called CATextLayer. The text layer is good for doing most of the text-related layout we'd want to do. It is not a full-fledged layout engine for text, though, so if you want to put text on a path, you will have to resort to using some more advanced techniques (we will look at doing just that later in this chapter). Next set the string and name for the layer. The string property contains the string that will be rendered. Next we set the font and the foregroundColor (again, the color is a Quartz color, and we will look at the code shortly).

Next up we do a bit more layout math. This is necessary until we get a chance to get into the layout management features in the next section. For now, the important thing to note in the last bit of this code is the preferredSize method. The CATextLayer uses the font and string to calculate how big the layer should be to fully display all the text. This saves us a lot of code and hassle because although it's not hard to figure out how much space a string needs, it's tedious, error-prone code.

And finally let's take a look at the code to create the colors we have been using:

CoreAnimation/SimpleMenu/MyController.m

```
Line 1    - (CGColorSpaceRef)genericRGBSpace {
      -       static CGColorSpaceRef space = NULL;
      -       if(NULL == space) {
      -         space = CGColorSpaceCreateWithName (kCGColorSpaceGenericRGB);
      5       }
      -       return space;
      -    }
      -
      -    - (CGColorRef)black {
      10      static CGColorRef black = NULL;
      -       if(black == NULL) {
      -         CGFloat values[4] = {0.0, 0.0, 0.0, 1.0};
      -         black = CGColorCreate([self genericRGBSpace], values);
      -       }
      15      return black;
      -    }
```

The genericRGBSpace method on line 1 creates (if necessary) and then returns the generic color red, green, blue (RGB) color space. A color space defines the boundaries of what colors can be expressed, and the generic RGB space is good for onscreen colors. If you are doing something more sophisticated, you might want to look at the different options on color spaces. Next up is the black method on line 1, which creates the color (again if necessary). I typically put this color creation code into a utility class so that I have to capture it in only one place.

Now we have seen our first layer-based user interface, it does not do much yet, but that is OK. Over the next several sections, we will be adding more and more features to this app so that we can get close to the look of Front Row. The next section covers how to lay out layers using the built-in layout mechanisms as well as how to create our own layout scheme. We will use the layout manager to simplify our code before we dive into scrolling.

7.4 Layer Layout with Constraints

As we saw in the previous example, we can easily lay out our layers manually. Although the code is simple, it is tedious and error prone. Another aspect to the manual layout from the previous example that we did not discuss is the resizing of the view (and thus the root layer). When the root layer is resized, the layers that we manually laid out will not resize or move. Instead, our layout will start to look pretty strange. The most straightforward way out of this mess is to use an instance of CAConstraintLayoutManager to constrain our layers to fit together nicely. In this section, we will see how this class is used to ensure that our layers are consistently looking like we want even when the layer is resized. In addition to making dealing with resizing easier, a layout manager also simplifies our layout code considerably. Let's take a look at how this stuff works.

The CAConstraintLayoutManager works on a principle of constraining various properties of layers to other layers. The idea is similar to the size inspector in Interface Builder for views, sides, widths, and so on, that can be "locked" together. There are eight properties used in the CAConstraintLayoutManager constraint system arranged along the horizontal axis and the vertical axis (four constraints each axis). The horizontal axis constraints are shown in Figure 7.3, on the facing page.

The horizontal axis constraints allow us to control the layout of our layers along that axis. Similarly, we have the vertical axis constraints that allow us to control the vertical layout of our layers (see Figure 7.4, on page 88).

Together these constraints give us extensive control over the layout of the layers in our applications. Each of these constraints represents a conceptual point on the layer that can be attached to another conceptual point on another layer (either a sibling or a parent in the layer tree). As an example, we can constrain two sibling layers to have the same minimum x value by constraining both of their kCAConstraintMinX constraints to their superlayers' kCAConstraintMinX attribute.

Layout is not directly invoked on layers. Instead, we call the method setNeedsLayout (or it is called on our behalf by the layer when a change requires it). Calling the setNeedsLayout method "schedules" the layer for layout and causes the layout manager to be invoked on the next pass through the event loop. Although typically this detail is unimportant to us, sometimes we have to be aware of the timing of the actual layout

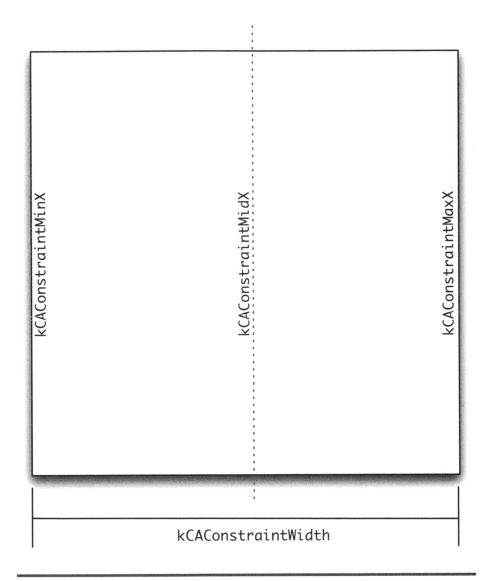

Figure 7.3: X-AXIS CONSTRAINTS

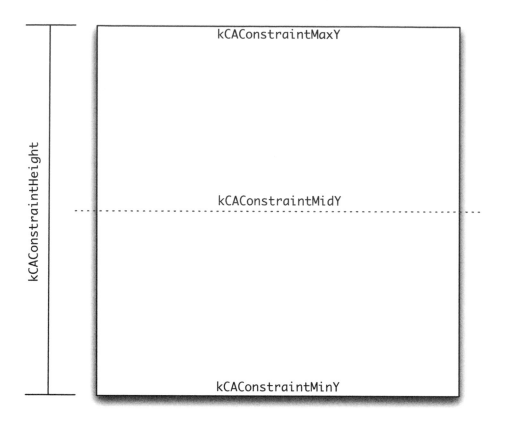

Figure 7.4: Y Axis Constraints

happening. It is most often an issue while starting up an application. One of the examples later in this chapter will discuss these issues in more detail. In the meantime, the best way to gain an understanding of layout is to see some code:

CoreAnimation/SimpleMenuLayout/MyControllerLayout.m

```
Line 1   - (void)awakeFromNib {
    -        CALayer *layer = [CALayer layer];
    -        layer.backgroundColor = [self black];
    -        layer.layoutManager = [CAConstraintLayoutManager layoutManager];
    5        [view setLayer:layer];
    -        [view setWantsLayer:YES];
    -        [view.layer addSublayer:[self menuLayer]];
    -    }
```

The awakeFromNib method has not changed much from the previous example. All we added was layoutManager on line 4. This is what associates the layout manager with the layer. Now any sublayers that are added with constraints (we will see them next) will be automatically laid out by this manager:

`CoreAnimation/SimpleMenuLayout/MyControllerLayout.m`

```
Line 1   - (CALayer *)menuLayer {
   -       CGFloat offset = 10.0f;
   -       CALayer *menu = [CALayer layer];
   -       menu.name = @"menu";
   5       [menu addConstraint:
   -        [CAConstraint constraintWithAttribute:kCAConstraintMinX
   -                              relativeTo:@"superlayer"
   -                              attribute:kCAConstraintMidX]];
   -       [menu addConstraint:
  10        [CAConstraint constraintWithAttribute:kCAConstraintMaxX
   -                              relativeTo:@"superlayer"
   -                              attribute:kCAConstraintMaxX offset:-offset]];
   -       [menu addConstraint:
   -        [CAConstraint constraintWithAttribute:kCAConstraintMinY
  15                              relativeTo:@"superlayer"
   -                              attribute:kCAConstraintMinY offset:offset]];
   -       [menu addConstraint:
   -        [CAConstraint constraintWithAttribute:kCAConstraintMaxY
   -                              relativeTo:@"superlayer"
  20                              attribute:kCAConstraintMaxY offset:-offset]];
   -       menu.borderWidth = 2.0f;
   -       menu.borderColor = [self white];
   -       menu.layoutManager = [CAConstraintLayoutManager layoutManager];
   -
  25       NSArray *names = [NSArray arrayWithObjects:
   -                         @"Option 1", @"Option 2", @"Option 3", nil];
   -       NSArray *items = [self menuItemsFromNames:names
   -                                    offset:offset];
   -       [menu setSublayers:items];
  30
   -       return menu;
   -   }
```

Next let's take a look at the menuLayer method to see the constraints in action. This method has been changed only to replace the NSRect-based layout with a constraints-based layout. Notice our first constraint on line 8. This constraint says that the menu layer's minimum x value should be constrained relative to the mid x point in its superlayer. Put another way, this is saying that the left edge of the menu layer should be on the midpoint of the root layer. The next constraint is constraining the maximum x value of the menu layer to be coincident with the maximum x value of the superlayer (the root layer in this case). With the additional argument of offset, we are also saying that the constraint should be enforced but offset by the argument's value. Next up is the creation of the menu item layers:

CoreAnimation/SimpleMenuLayout/MyControllerLayout.m

```
- (NSArray *)menuItemsFromNames:(NSArray *)itemNames
                        offset:(CGFloat)offset {
  NSMutableArray *menuItems = [NSMutableArray array];
  NSFont *font = [NSFont boldSystemFontOfSize:18.0f];
  int counter = 0;
  for(NSString *itemName in itemNames) {
    CATextLayer *layer = [CATextLayer layer];
    layer.string = itemName;
    layer.name = itemName;
    layer.foregroundColor = [self white];
    layer.font = font;
    layer.alignmentMode = kCAAlignmentCenter;
    [layer addConstraint:
     [CAConstraint constraintWithAttribute:kCAConstraintMidX
                             relativeTo:@"superlayer"
                              attribute:kCAConstraintMidX]];
    [layer addConstraint:
     [CAConstraint constraintWithAttribute:kCAConstraintWidth
                             relativeTo:@"superlayer"
                              attribute:kCAConstraintWidth
                                 offset:-2.0f * offset]];
    if(counter == 0) {
      [layer addConstraint:
       [CAConstraint constraintWithAttribute:kCAConstraintMaxY
                               relativeTo:@"superlayer"
                                attribute:kCAConstraintMaxY
                                   offset:-offset]];
    } else {
      NSString *previousLayerName = [itemNames objectAtIndex:counter - 1];
      [layer addConstraint:
       [CAConstraint constraintWithAttribute:kCAConstraintMaxY
                               relativeTo:previousLayerName
                                attribute:kCAConstraintMinY
                                   offset:-offset]];
    }
    [menuItems addObject:layer];
    counter++;
  }
  return menuItems;
}
```

The menuItemsFromNames:offset: method has been changed to remove the size argument. We no longer need it to do the layout. The first two constraints are configuring the horizontal axis for the menu items. Since all of them will have the same location along the horizontal axis, we can configure each item the same way. Next up we have to make a special case for the first item because it's tied to the menu layer on the vertical axis. And finally, we constrain each of the rest of the items to the layer that is just previous to it. The important thing to note (besides the constraints, of course) here is that we are using the previous layer's name as the relativeTo: argument. This is where naming layers becomes important for more than debugging. That name is the same name we attached to the layer earlier by specifying the name property.

If you are counting, you might have noticed that there are few more lines of code here than in the previous example. These additional three or four lines of code allow the layer to be resized. The layout remains constant where possible (in other words, if the layer shrinks, too much the text won't be able to fully display).

In this chapter, we have covered a lot of introductory ground. Layers live in a tree that has a defined 3D coordinate space. These objects have a particular geometry that can be configured and constrained via the CAConstraintLayoutManager or a layout manager of our own design. We have only begun to scratch the surface of what we can do with layers. In Chapter 10, *Layers in 3D*, on page 131, we will continue to develop our Front Row–like application and start building some of the animation and 3D effects into the app so that we can gain experience with some of the more powerful aspects of layers.

Now that we have seen layout managers in action and talked through how to configure them, it's time to move on to scrolling. Adding scrolling does increase the complexity of our application a bit, but it gives us the ability to manage more content in a sensible and straightforward way. Conceptually scrolling with Core Animation is the same as scrolling in AppKit. The details differ a bit. The scrolling APIs for layers are a bit lower level, but they are straightforward to pick up.

I think, at a child's birth, if a mother could ask a fairy godmother to endow it with the most useful gift, that gift should be curiosity.

► Eleanor Roosevelt

Chapter 8

Core Animation Layers

In the previous chapter, we discussed layer-hosting views. We'll continue along those lines and introduce new functionality as well as look at some of the deeper aspects of what we have already covered. In this chapter, you'll find that some of what we learned earlier when discussing layer-backed views and animation types will apply almost directly to layers (where it does not, I'll cover the details). Other things such as the CAMediaTiming protocol have not been covered yet at all. As this chapter progresses, you will understand the details behind layers and the animations we apply to them on a whole new level.

8.1 Animation Types and Layers

Let's start by understanding how to apply what you have learned thus far to a purely layer-based approach. We will revisit an old example with a twist. We are gong to take the example we did in Section 3.2, *Keyframe Animations*, on page 22 and make it layer-based. You will see the differences both great and small between that really simple app created with AppKit and the same app created with layers. Since much of the code is the same between the two approaches, we will be discussing only the differences, with a brief mention of the similar code.

One of the differences between the layer-based animation and the view-based animation is that we can't use the NSImageView class to hold our image. We instead need to create a CGImageRef that we can pass into our layer as its contents property (we will talk more about the layer's contents property later in this chapter).

Thankfully, it is straightforward:

CoreAnimationLayers/AnimationTypes/MyView.m

```
Line 1    - (CGImageRef)beach {
            if(beach == NULL) {
              NSString *path = [[NSBundle mainBundle] pathForResource:@"beach"
                                                               ofType:@"jpg"];
     5        NSURL *beachURL = [NSURL fileURLWithPath:path];
              CGImageSourceRef src = CGImageSourceCreateWithURL((CFURLRef)beachURL, NULL);
              if(NULL != src) {
                beach = CGImageSourceCreateImageAtIndex(src, 0, NULL);
                CFRelease(src);
    10        }
            }
            return beach;
          }
```

In the beach method, we are getting the beach.jpg file out of our application's bundle and loading it as a CGImageRef. First we locate the file on line 4; then we create the URL on line 5. This URL is then cast to a CFURLRef (which works like a champ because of toll-free bridging) and used to create a CGImageSourceRef. Then if all has gone well to this point, we create a image via the CGImageSourceCreateImageAtIndex() function. A full discussion of the details of CGImage is beyond the scope of this book, so we won't go into too much more detail. However, the Quartz book ([GL06]) is a great resource to help you dive deep into CGImages.

Now that we have our image, we can set the contents property of a layer. Let's take a look at that code now:

CoreAnimationLayers/AnimationTypes/MyView.m

```
Line 1    - (CALayer *)photoLayer {
            if(nil == photoLayer) {
              photoLayer = [CALayer layer];
              photoLayer.contents = (id)self.beach;
     5        photoLayer.bounds = CGRectMake(0.0f, 0.0f, 280.0f, 210.0f);
              photoLayer.position = CGPointMake(NSMidX([self bounds]),
                                                NSMidY([self bounds]));
              photoLayer.name = @"photo";
              [self.layer addSublayer:photoLayer];
    10      }
            return photoLayer;
          }
```

In this method, we are creating a layer to hold our photo. This is the layer that we will eventually animate. Notice that on line 4 we are setting the contents property of our view. When the contents is set to a

CGImageRef, the image becomes what the layer draws. A layer can draw in much the same way a view can (the method is called drawInContext: instead of drawRect:, but the concept is similar). However, it is much more typical to set the contents of the layer or to draw into the layer via delegation (with the drawLayer:inContext: method) than it is to subclass CALayer. Notice also that we are setting the bounds and the position of this layer. The default value for both properties is zero for each member (in other words, the bounds defaults to ({{0.0f, 0.0f}, {0.0f, 0.0f}})). Since the bounds defaults to zero, you won't see the layer unless you change the bounds.

Next we call the photoLayer method from the awakeFromNib method. Let's look at that code now:

```
CoreAnimationLayers/AnimationTypes/MyView.m
```

```
- (void)awakeFromNib {
    [self setLayer:[CALayer layer]];
    self.layer.backgroundColor = [self black];
    [self setWantsLayer:YES];
    [self photoLayer];
}
```

In this method we are creating the layer that our view hosts and setting its background color. We also call the photoLayer method that causes our photo layer to be created and added as a sublayer. This is different from the way we worked with views. Recall that in the keyframe example in Chapter 3, *Animation Types*, on page 21 we created an NSImageView and added it as a subview in the initWithFrame: method. Although using initWithFrame: is a good place to configure a view hierarchy, it's not the best place to configure the layer hierarchy in a layer-hosting view. When a view is loaded from a NIB file, it is sent initWithFrame: early in the loading cycle, and as it is read out of the NIB file (later in the cycle), its properties are set, including wantsLayer. So, the wantsLayer property will (by default) get set to NO as the view is loaded from the NIB file, after we have configured the layer hierarchy in initWithFrame:, which will cause our layer and the whole hierarchy to be removed. To make sure that does not happen, you should configure your layers in the awake-FromNib method of your custom view. It is kind of confusing when you are staring at your blank view, but all the code looks right, so keep this in mind as you write your layer hierarchy configuration code.

The path for the animation and the creation of the animation do not change from the view-based approach to the layer-based approach.

CoreAnimationLayers/AnimationTypes/MyView.m

```
- (CGPathRef)heartPath {
  CGPoint position = [photoLayer position];
  if(heartPath == NULL) {
    CGFloat offset = 50.0f;
    heartPath = CGPathCreateMutable();
    CGPathMoveToPoint(heartPath, NULL, position.x, position.y);
    CGPathAddLineToPoint(heartPath, NULL, position.x - offset,
                         position.y + offset);
    CGPathAddLineToPoint(heartPath, NULL, position.x,
                         position.y - 2.0f * offset);
    CGPathAddLineToPoint(heartPath, NULL, position.x + offset,
                         position.y + offset);
    CGPathAddLineToPoint(heartPath, NULL, position.x, position.y);
    CGPathCloseSubpath(heartPath);
  }
  return heartPath;
}

- (CAKeyframeAnimation *)positionAnimation {
  if(nil == positionAnimation) {
    positionAnimation = [CAKeyframeAnimation animation];
    positionAnimation.path = self.heartPath;
    positionAnimation.duration = 2.0f;
    positionAnimation.calculationMode = kCAAnimationPaced;
    [positionAnimation retain];
  }
  return positionAnimation;
}
```

If you take a look at the code in Section 3.2, *Keyframe Animations*, on page 22, you can see that this is the same code except that the animation has been renamed positionAnimation since we are animating the position of the layer instead of the origin. A layer has a frame property, but unlike a view, it is derived from position, bounds, anchorPoint, and transform. Just another point of intuition development here: don't let it get you down; if something is not working the way you want or expect, remember that layers are slightly different in a few places, and you have to sometimes rethink what you are doing with the layer to see why it's not working as you expect.

Finally, let's take a look at the code to apply the animation:

CoreAnimationLayers/AnimationTypes/MyView.m

```
- (void)bounce {
  [self.photoLayer addAnimation:self.positionAnimation
   forKey:@"position"];
}
```

Notice that we directly add the animation to the layer via addAnimation:forKey: rather than set the animations dictionary as we did with views. This brings up another point about dealing with layers instead of views. Layers implicitly animate just about every property they have. When we set the position of a layer, it animates by default instead of us having to get a proxy as we did with views. Also, when we add an animation to a layer, it automatically starts as soon as it's added. In other words, calling addAnimation:forKey: starts an animation, whereas on a view when we set the animations dictionary, the view is animated only if the property that matches the key was changed. This is a subtle difference but is important to keep in mind. The same kind of functionality can be achieved with the actions dictionary in the layer; we will discuss that shortly.

Animating Layers and Events

In AppKit when we move a view around without the animator, we are in complete control of where the view is during any particular frame of the animation. When doing animation with layers, as we just saw, Core Animation takes over control of where the layer is during any particular frame. That of course saves us a bunch of code and complexity, but occasionally we need to know where the layer is so that we can perform hit testing or other event processing. That is where the presentationLayer comes in.

The presentation layer of any layer is a read-only copy of the layer that is a very close approximation of what the layer looked like at the start of the current frame in the animation. So, for example, you might have a game where the user is supposed to click moving images. As the user clicks, you would use the presentation layer to determine whether the layer was hit. Although our example is not a game, it will serve as a good example of how to use the presentation layer for event processing. Let's look at the code to see how we process events in a layer-based UI:

CoreAnimationLayers/AnimationTypes/MyView.m

```
Line 1   - (void)mouseDown:(NSEvent *)event {
             NSPoint point = [self convertPoint:[event locationInWindow] fromView:nil];
             CALayer *presLayer = [self.photoLayer presentationLayer];
             CALayer *layer = [presLayer hitTest:NSPointToCGPoint(point)];
      5      if([layer.name isEqualToString:@"photo"]) {
               NSBeep();
             }
         }
```

The hitTest: method call on line 4 finds the layer (either presLayer or one of its sublayers) that is hit by the point. Now that the hit layer is known, we can do whatever event processing we want to do. In this case, we are simply beeping if the user hits the layer, but in the next great game that you are writing, hitting the layer might lead to the high score. Notice that the clicked point is converted from an NSPoint to a CGPoint. All the Core Animation APIs take CG types so when we are crossing over from an NSView to a CALayer, we almost always have to do this type of conversion.

The layer is now animating around the path in the same way we had it animating in our previous example.

8.2 Animation Timing

Back in Chapter 4, *Animation Timing*, on page 39, we saw how to customize the timing of an animation by setting a timing function or specifying one of the built-in timing curves using the timingFunction property. You can use this same approach with layers and get the same effects. However, there is so much more you can do with animation than set its timingFunction. In fact, the CAAnimation class implements the CAMediaTiming protocol, which gives us a model for a hierarchal timing coordinate system. Similar to the way each view in a view hierarchy has its own coordinate system for drawing, each animation can have its own time coordinate system. The timing coordinate system gives us amazing flexibility and power in arranging and timing animations. In this section, we are going to go into the detail behind the CAMediaTiming protocol and how we can use its properties to make our animations do amazing things.

This is all a bit abstract without an example. So, let's talk through a potential case for using this more advanced timing functionality. Let's say you are building a photo-viewing application and you want the photos to slide across the scene and fade in and out as they do so. Using the control you gain from the CAMediaTiming properties will allow you to specify exactly when the fade starts. The fade does not need to start at the same time as the slide. We could also slide multiple images across the screen at the same time and have them all offset from one another. Shortly we will go over an example application that does similar things to make this concept even more concrete.

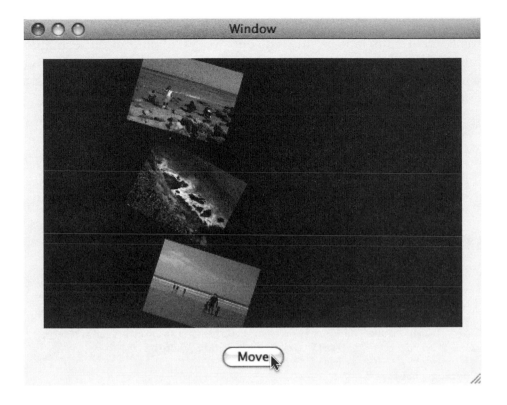

Figure 8.1: POPVIEW APPLICATION

Since the time coordinate system is a line instead of a two- or three-dimensional coordinate system, the transformations we can do to it are simpler. The CAMediaTiming protocol defines the properties that control these timeline transformations. They fall into two basic groups, scaling and offsetting. The scaling of the timeline is controlled by the speed and duration attributes, and the offset of the timeline is controlled by the beginTime and timeOffset properties. The fillMode property lets us specify what state an animation should take when we change the offset of the timeline. We can exert almost complete control over the way an animation plays out by manipulating these values.

Let's build a simple application that pushes three photos across the scene, fades them in and out, and rotates them as they move, as shown in Figure 8.1.

In this application we have four animations going on: translate across the scene, rotate, fade in, and fade out. We put all four of these animations into a group (an instance of CAAnimationGroup) and then add that animation group to the layer. Here is the code invoked from the Move button in the UI:

CoreAnimationLayers/PhotoPop/PopView.m

```
- (IBAction)move:(id)sender {
  [beach1Layer addAnimation:[self group] forKey:@"fly"];
  [beach2Layer addAnimation:[self group] forKey:@"fly"];
  [beach3Layer addAnimation:[self group] forKey:@"fly"];
}
```

For completeness, here's how you create the group animation:

CoreAnimationLayers/PhotoPop/PopView.m

```
- (CAAnimationGroup *)group {
  CAAnimationGroup *group = [CAAnimationGroup animation];
  group.duration = kGroupDuration;
  group.animations = [NSArray arrayWithObjects:[self rotation],
                      [self xLocation], [self fadeIn],
                      [self fadeOut], nil];

  return group;
}
```

This code is similar to how we created a group animation in earlier examples. We simply set the duration and add the four animations.

Because we want the rotation of the photos to be different across each layer, we need to offset the rotation by a little bit for each layer. Let's look at the code used in this example to stagger the rotations:

CoreAnimationLayers/PhotoPop/PopView.m

```
Line 1  - (CAKeyframeAnimation *)rotation {
          CAKeyframeAnimation *rot =
          [CAKeyframeAnimation animationWithKeyPath:@"transform.rotation"];
          CGFloat angle = 30.0f * (M_PI/180.0f);
     5    rot.values = [NSArray arrayWithObjects:[NSNumber numberWithFloat:0.0f],
                        [NSNumber numberWithFloat:angle],
                        [NSNumber numberWithFloat:-angle],
                        [NSNumber numberWithFloat:0.0f], nil];
          rot.keyTimes = [NSArray arrayWithObjects:[NSNumber numberWithFloat:0.0f],
    10                      [NSNumber numberWithFloat:0.25f],
                            [NSNumber numberWithFloat:0.75f],
                            [NSNumber numberWithFloat:1.0f], nil];
          rot.timeOffset = [self randomNumberLessThan:2.0f];
          return rot;
    15  }
```

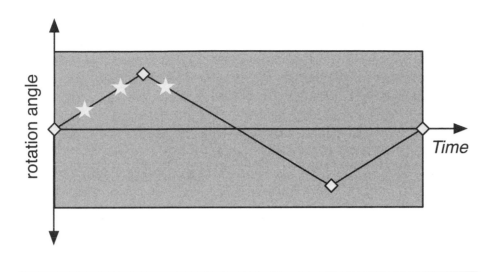

Figure 8.2: ROTATION ANIMATION TIMEOFFSET

The rotation is a straightforward keyframe animation that has four keyframes: 0, 30 degrees, -30 degrees, and then back to zero. Notice on line 13 that the timeOffset property is being set to a random number less than 2. So, each of the layers will have a slightly different offset to its rotation animation. We could have randomized the start and stop angles instead of using timeOffset, but that would have defeated the purpose of the example.

The timeOffset property conceptually moves the beginning of time for an animation to the time offset value. Recall that Core Animation is time-based (not frame-based), and the value for any particular property (such as rotation angle in our example) is determined based on time, not the frame. When we specify a time offset, we are moving forward in time for that animation. So, in this example, the rotation is starting at a random amount of time into the future of the animation (in this case, a random number less than two seconds). When we first see the animation, the value of the rotation is appropriate for the timeOffset assigned to the animation. In Figure 8.2, we see the rotation animation as it moves from +30 degrees to -30 degrees. There are three stars placed at potential timeOffset values for the three different layers. Let's return to our discussion of interpolation for a moment to better understand this.

Remember, Core Animation is going to smoothly interpolate between the values based on the timing function. Since we have specified key times here, the rotation angle will be smoothly interpolated between zero radians and angle radians at 0.25 of the duration, between "angle" and "-angle" at 0.75 of the duration, and finally -angle back to zero at the full duration. When we specify a time offset, the animation starts that far into the "future" of the animation.

To make the math easy, let's say our time offset random value is 0.25 into the animation (the duration of the group is 5 seconds, and since we did not change the rotation animation, its duration is also 5 seconds, so the timeOffset value would be 0.25 * 5.0 or 1.25 seconds). Because that time value corresponds directly to a keyTime, the value would be whatever value is specified at that key time. That would yield a rotation amount of "angle." So, for this animation, the photo would start out rotated "angle" radians. Then as the animation progresses, the values are calculated based on the adjusted (the adjustment is like a translation) time scale. So when the parent duration reaches half, our rotation would be at 0.75 of its time base for the purposes of doing the interpolation (for our rotation that would put the photo rotated to "-angle"). Then as the group reaches 1.0 of its duration, the rotation goes back to 0.25 of its time base, so the interpolated value would be back to "angle." This has the effect of looking like the animation is in a loop, starting some time in the future of the animation and ending at that same future point.

I specifically chose to do the timeOffset with the rotation angle because the effects of the "wraparound" are not as obvious with this animation as they would be with something like the xPosition (which we will look at shortly). If you want a better visual of the wraparound effect, you can add a timeOffset value to the xPosition animation. The visual effect is more dramatic, making it much easier to see.

Now let's look at the fadeIn animation. To make the fade-in work, we start with a zero opacity and then ramp that up to one in a basic animation. Here is the code:

CoreAnimationLayers/PhotoPop/PopView.m

```
Line 1    - (CABasicAnimation *)fadeIn {
              CABasicAnimation *fade = [CABasicAnimation animationWithKeyPath:@"opacity"];
              fade.fromValue = [NSNumber numberWithFloat:0.0f];
              fade.toValue = [NSNumber numberWithFloat:1.0f];
       5      fade.speed = kGroupDuration;
              fade.fillMode = kCAFillModeForwards;
              return fade;
          }
```

The first thing to notice in this code is that we are setting the speed of the animation on line 5. The speed is set to the duration of the group. Recall that the speed is a scaling factor. Since the fadeIn animation is supposed to take one second, setting the speed to the duration of the group will make sure that the fadeIn always takes one second regardless of how long we make the group's duration. In other words, since the duration of the group is five seconds and the speed of the fadeIn is set to 5, what would normally take five seconds to complete will take only one second because it happens five times faster.

On line 6, the fillMode property is set to kCAFillModeForwards. That makes the fadeIn animation's final value continue to be applied after the duration of the animation ends. In contrast, by default the animation's effect will be removed from the layer when the animation completes. When the animation is removed, the value (opacity in this example) will return to its previous value (transparent in this case) and will disappear. Setting the fillMode to kCAFillModeForwards will cause the effect of the animation to remain even after the animation concludes.

fillMode can be set to one of four values. The default is kCAFillModeRemoved and specifies that the animation be removed when complete. The second kCAFillModeForwards we just discussed causes the final value of the animation to continue to be applied until the parent (in our example the group) completes its animation. The next is kCAFillModeBackawards, which causes the initial value of the animation to be applied from the starting time of the parent until the animation starts. And finally, we can specify kCAFillModeBoth to get the animation's initial value to apply until it starts and the final value to continue until its parent finishes.

Finally, let's look at the fadeOut animation. Here is the code:

`CoreAnimationLayers/PhotoPop/PopView.m`

```
Line 1   - (CABasicAnimation *)fadeOut {
    -        CABasicAnimation *fade = [CABasicAnimation animationWithKeyPath:@"opacity"];
    -        fade.fromValue = [NSNumber numberWithFloat:1.0f];
    -        fade.toValue = [NSNumber numberWithFloat:0.0f];
    5        fade.duration = kFadeDuration;
    -        fade.beginTime = kGroupDuration - kFadeDuration;
    -        return fade;
    -    }
```

In this code, we are using the same CABasicAnimation to fade from fully opaque down to fully transparent. Notice in this method that the beginTime property is set so the fadeOut happens over the last second of the group animation. When we specify a beginTime, it changes the time that the animation starts. The fade-out animation should finish as the group animation ends, and setting the beginTime makes that possible.

Two other groups of properties on the CAMediaTiming protocol can be used for some great effects. First, we can specify that an animation repeats, either a number of times with the repeatCount property or for a length of time with the repeatDuration property (we have to be careful, though, and specify only one or the other; if both are specified, the results are undefined). An animation can also be automatically reversed when it finishes by setting the autoreverses property. When you run the code, make sure to tweak these properties as well to get a feel for what is possible.

8.3 Rotation and Layers

As we saw with the previous example, it is easy to rotate layers. What we did not talk about in the previous example or at all yet is the location in the layer that the rotation is applied around. By default the center is used as the rotation point, but we can change this by changing the anchorPoint. In this section we will talk about rotation and how the look of it is changed by varying the anchor point.

In Figure 8.3, on the next page, we see a screen shot of an application we will use to explore the anchorPoint and rotation.

In this shot we have left the anchorPoint at the default. Now let's look at the code and see how the anchor point works with the rotation. Here is the code:

CoreAnimationLayers/LayerRotate/PhotoRotateView.m

```
- (IBAction)rotate:(id)sender {
    [beachLayer setValue:[NSNumber numberWithFloat:(30.0f * M_PI / 180.0f)]
            forKeyPath:@"transform.rotation"];
}
```

We simply have to call setValue:forKeyPath: with the *transform.rotation* key path. We could also create a rotation called CATransform3D with the CATransform3DMakeRotation() function and set that to get the transform of our layer. Since this takes fewer lines of code, we will use the setValue:forKeyPath: method in these examples. Since we have not changed the anchorPoint, the layer rotates around its center (which is what is in the earlier screen shot). Now let's look at changing the anchor point.

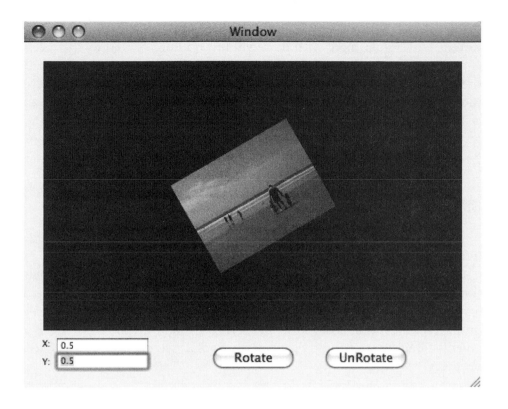

Figure 8.3: ROTATE LAYER

CoreAnimationLayers/LayerRotate/PhotoRotateView.m

```
Line 1   - (IBAction)setXAnchorPoint:(id)sender {
    -        CGFloat newValue = [sender floatValue];
    -        if(newValue >= 0.0f && newValue <= 1.0f) {
    -          beachLayer.anchorPoint = CGPointMake(newValue, beachLayer.anchorPoint.y);
    5        } else {
    -          NSBeep();
    -          [sender setFloatValue:0.5f];
    -        }
    -      }
    10
    -      - (IBAction)setYAnchorPoint:(id)sender {
    -        CGFloat newValue = [sender floatValue];
    -        if(newValue >= 0.0f && newValue <= 1.0f) {
    -          beachLayer.anchorPoint = CGPointMake(beachLayer.anchorPoint.x, newValue);
    15       } else {
    -          NSBeep();
    -          [sender setFloatValue:0.5f];
    -        }
    -      }
```

On line 4, we change the x value of the anchor point, and we change the y on line 14. Experiment with these values, and notice that as the value is changed, not only does the rotation point change but the location of the layer changes as well. Recall that the anchor point is the spot where the layer's position is tied to, so when the anchor point is changed, so is the relative location of the position. Spend some time changing the anchorPoint and rotating and unrotating the layer to see how the anchor point affects the rotation.

8.4 Filters and Layers

As you recall from Chapter 6, *Filtered Views*, on page 63, Core Image filters can be used with Core Animation to add GPU-accelerated effects to images. You read about applying these filters to views, and the great thing is that everything you learned there applies directly to layers. In a view, you apply a filter to the background with the backgroundFilters property, and you use the same property with a layer. The content of a layer is filtered with the filters property, where a view has the contentFilters property.

The filters applied to layers are animated in the same way that they were when animating filters on views. All you need to do is name your filter (remember, it's the name property, not the name used to create the filter), and then you can animate any of its parameters via its key path (that is, filters.blurFilter.inputIntensity, assuming the name of your filter is blurFilter).

The typical use of these filters is to put a blur filter on to layers that are supposed to appear to be more in the background. But there are many many filters to experiment with. Try them on your UI and see which ones fit. Be careful not to overwhelm your users. It is much better to be subtle.

8.5 Managing a Layer's Contents

To this point, we have mostly been dealing with putting images into layers via the contents property and letting the default setting stay. In this section, we will look at the ways we can place and otherwise control the content of our layers.

The contentsGravity property on the layer lets us tell the layer where we want the content relative to the layer. The default is kCAGravityResize, which causes the content to be resized to fill the layer's bounds. We can also specify kCAGravityResizeAspectFill to get the content to fill the whole layer but preserve the content's aspect ratio. There are other options that allow us to place the content at the top, bottom, right, and left and combinations of these (top right, and so on). It is typical to use this attribute when a layer must be a particular size that is different from the content (for various reason this happens, but typically it is for layout reasons), especially when the layer is a different aspect ratio from the content and you don't want the content scaled.

8.6 Drawing in Layers

There are several ways we can get our content into a layer. We could draw the content we want in the layer into a custom CGBitmapContext and then get a CGImage from that context and place that as the contents. We can subclass CALayer, override the drawInContext: method, and draw our content into the context that is passed into us. Or we can provide a delegate and have that implement the method drawLayer:inContext: and do our drawing with the context passed to that method. Which approach you choose depends on your requirements or personal taste. I find creating a CGBitmapContext to be error prone, so I generally try to avoid that route. Subclassing CALayer is a good approach if you need a subclass anyway because of some other reason (you need to add data and functionality for your application). Overriding drawInContext: is natural in this context. I generally try to avoid creating subclasses of CALayer simply to do custom drawing but instead use the third approach of providing a delegate. My suggestion to you is to experiment with at least creating a subclass and providing a delegate to get comfortable with both approaches. In the examples in the rest of this section, we will be using the delegate method.

In this example, we will draw a rectangle into a layer. Let's first look at the code to set up the layer for our drawing:

CoreAnimationLayers/LayerDrawing/LayerDrawingView.m

```
Line 1  - (void)awakeFromNib {
     -      [self setLayer:[CALayer layer]];
     -      [self setWantsLayer:YES];
     -      self.layer.layoutManager = [CAConstraintLayoutManager layoutManager];
     5      self.layer.backgroundColor = [self black];
     -      self.drawingLayer.delegate = self;
     -      [self.drawingLayer setNeedsDisplay];
     -      NSUInteger resizeMask =  kCALayerWidthSizable | kCALayerHeightSizable;
     -      self.drawingLayer.autoresizingMask = resizeMask;
    10      self.drawingLayer.needsDisplayOnBoundsChange = YES;
     -      [self.layer addSublayer:self.drawingLayer];
     -  }
```

Here we're doing the typical stuff we've done many times before: creating a layer and setting it as the layer for our view, setting a constraints-based layout manager, and setting the background color. Then comes the important code for our purposes here. On line 6, we set the delegate of our drawing layer to the view (typically you'd have a different class be the delegate), and then on line 7 we tell the layer that it needs to be drawn. This is a spot where layers distinctly perform differently than views. When a view is created, it automatically "needs display," whereas a layer assumes that it does not. So when the layer is created, if we are planning on drawing into it, we must tell it that it needs to be displayed. Next on line 9, we set the resizing mask. By default a layer will not resize when its superlayer resizes, and setting this mask will change that. There are several options I have specified here so the sublayer will resize its width and height as the superlayer resizes (thus staying the same relative size). You should change the values, though, and see how the others affect the layer. And finally on line 10, the layer is being told to display when its bounds change. This is another point of departure from views: when a view is resized, it automatically redraws, but a layer does not. Remember that Core Animation is optimized to do animation and thus avoids drawing whenever it can. When we force a redraw, the backing store must be updated, which is a relatively expensive operation, so redraw only if you must.

8.7 Tiled Layers

The tiled layer is a way for you to manage or represent content that is too big too fit into a layer. The size of a layer is dependent on the graphics card on the computer that the software is running on, but generally a 2048 by 2048 image will fit without problem into a layer on a typical Leopard-era Mac. If you have images that are larger than that (say 10000 by 10000), then you will have to use a CATiledLayer to display this content at its full resolution.

The example we are going to use to illustrate the tiled layer is a panoramic image composed of about 16 photos for a total resolution of 9162 pixels wide by 4367 pixels high. The image was sliced into 24 equally sized segments of 1527 pixels wide by 1094 pixels high. In this application I presliced the image, but in a real application you would probably want to load the file incrementally (see the [GL06] Quartz book for more detail), or you could slice it up programmatically (see Section 12.2, *Layers and Animations*, on page 166 for an example). Let's first look at the setup of our tiled layer.

Here's the code:

```
Line 1   photoLayer = [CATiledLayer layer];
    -    TiledDelegate *delegate = [[TiledDelegate alloc] init];
    -    photoLayer.delegate = delegate;
    -    zoomLevel = 1.0f;
    5    photoLayer.frame = CGRectMake(0.0f, 0.0f, delegate.imageSize.width,
    -                                     delegate.imageSize.height);
    -    // set the levels of detail (range is 2^-2 to 2^1)
    -    photoLayer.levelsOfDetail = 4;
    -    // set the bias for how many 'zoom in' levels there are
    10   photoLayer.levelsOfDetailBias = 1; // up to 2x (2^1)of the largest photo
    -    [photoLayer setNeedsDisplay]; // display the whole layer
```

We create the layer as we would any other layer—by invoking the layer class method. Next we create an instance of TiledDelegate and set the layer's delegate on line 3. The delegate for a tiled layer is particularly important because it is responsible for doing all the drawing required by the tiled layer. If you were to set the tiled layer's contents to an image (as we do with other layers), then the tiled layer would revert to a "normal" layer. We will look at the drawing code shortly.

Next, the default zoomLevel value is set to 1.0, and the frame of the photoLayer is set to the size of the image. The zoomLevel is used to set the scale transformation on the photo layer. We will see how to use this property shortly. The frame of the photoLayer is set to the full resolution size of the image.

Next we set the levelsOfDetail property on line 8. The levelsOfDetail determines how many levels the tiled layer will cache. Next we set the levelsOfDetailBias, and that specifies how many levels of detail beyond one are reserved for zooming out. So, the configuration we have here specifies that we have four levels of detail ranging from 2^{-2} to 2^1; or, in other words, the image can be drawn at 25%, 50%, 100%, and 200%.

In Figure 8.4, on the following page, you can see the image zoomed out to 25% of its original size. And in the next image, Figure 8.5, on the next page, you can see the same image zoomed in to twice its original size.

This bigger image is much more detailed; we can see the texture of the paint on the fence and the detail of the grass. But at this level of detail, the image is much too large to fit into a layer. The tiled layer gives us the means to display this image simply even though it is way too big.

Figure 8.4: TILED LAYER ZOOMED OUT

Figure 8.5: TILED LAYER ZOOMED IN

Next, let's look at moving the image via the moveRight: method. Here is the code:

CoreAnimationLayers/TiledLayer/MyView.m

```
- (void)moveRight:(id)sender {
  CGFloat zoomFactor = zoomLevel > 1.0f ? zoomLevel : 1.0f / zoomLevel;
  CGFloat newXPos = photoLayer.position.x - (10.0f * zoomFactor);
  if(newXPos > (CGRectGetMaxX(photoLayer.superlayer.bounds) -
                CGRectGetWidth(photoLayer.frame) * photoLayer.anchorPoint.x)) {
    photoLayer.position = CGPointMake(newXPos, photoLayer.position.y);
  }
}
```

Since this view is the first responder, this method is called when the right arrow is pushed. In this code we are moving the position of the layer to the left 10 pixels at a time. We also check to see whether scrolling would move the layer past the left edge of the superlayer and stop scrolling if the layer has reached that point. Apart from the checks for scrolling past the edge, this code is remarkably simple. We did not have to write any code to deal with loading the image here or dealing with what is cached or what is not cached. The tiled layer takes care of all that for us. Next let's look at the code to draw the image. Here's the drawing code:

CoreAnimationLayers/TiledLayer/TiledDelegate.m

```
Line 1  - (void)drawLayer:(CALayer *)layer inContext:(CGContextRef)ctx {
          CGRect bounds = CGContextGetClipBoundingBox(ctx);
          NSInteger leftColumn = floor(CGRectGetMinX(bounds) / self.sliceSize.width);
          NSInteger bottomRow = floor(CGRectGetMinY(bounds) / self.sliceSize.height);
     5    NSInteger rightColumn = floor(CGRectGetMaxX(bounds) / self.sliceSize.width);
          NSInteger topRow = floor(CGRectGetMaxY(bounds) / self.sliceSize.height);
          NSInteger rowCount = topRow - bottomRow + 1;
          NSInteger columnCount = rightColumn - leftColumn + 1;
          for(int i = bottomRow;i < bottomRow + rowCount;i++) {
    10      for(int j = leftColumn;j < leftColumn + columnCount;j++) {
              CGPoint origin = CGPointMake(j * self.sliceSize.width,
                                           i * self.sliceSize.height);
              NSString *imgName = [NSString stringWithFormat:@"%dx%dy",
                                   (NSInteger)origin.x, (NSInteger)origin.y];
    15        CGImageRef image = [self imageNamed:imgName ofType:@"png"];
              if(NULL != image) {
                CGRect drawRect = CGRectMake(origin.x, origin.y, self.sliceSize.width,
                                             self.sliceSize.height);
                CGContextDrawImage(ctx, drawRect, image);

    20          CGImageRelease(image);
              }
            }
          }
    25  }
```

The most complex thing about this code is finding which tile to load and draw. Once we know what to load and draw, though, it's really simple to get the image to the screen. All we have to do is ask Quartz to do the drawing for us, as on 19.

There are some things to note about this code. We don't have to mess with scaling or cropping the image; all we have to do is draw it. This is one of the coolest things about the way the tiled layer works. The context that is passed into this method has already had all the transformations applied to get it into the correct state for us to draw to. All we have to do is draw.

Take a minute to run the application for yourself. Notice that as you move around the image, either with a scroll wheel on a mouse or with the arrow keys, the image incrementally loads in. The tiled layer knows what parts of the image have been loaded, and when a part that is not cached becomes visible, the layer will ask the delegate to draw by calling the drawLayer:inContext:. As the content is drawn into the context, it is cached by the layer so that it's ready to display when that area becomes visible again.

8.8 Animations and Actions

We first discussed the search pattern for animations in Section 2.3, *Finding Animations*, on page 15 in our discussion of Cocoa Animation. The search for animations in layers is similar, but there are a few more steps. In this section, I am going to talk about the search pattern and show you how to override the default animations.

The animation search starts with the layer's actionForKey: method. This in turn goes through several methods to find the animation to run. First the layer's delegate is sent actionForLayer:forKey:, which can return the animation to use, return nil to signify that the search should continue or return, or return NSNull to signify that the search should terminate. When you implement actionForLayer:forKey:, you can replace the default animation by returning your own animation, you can let the default search continue by return nil, or you can stop the search and prevent the default animation from running.

Here is some code that does all three options for different keys:

```
- (id<CAAction>)actionForLayer:(CALayer *)layer forKey:(NSString *)key {
  id<CAAction> action = nil;
  if([key isEqualToString:@"opacity"]) {
    CABasicAnimation *animation =
    [CABasicAnimation animationWithKeyPath:@"opacity"];
    animation.duration = 0.5f;
    action = animation;
  } else if([key isEqualToString:@"sublayers"]) {
    action = (id<CAAction>)[NSNull null];
  }
  return action;
}
```

For the opacity key, we replace the default animation with one that lasts for half a second (the default lasts 0.25 seconds). For the sublayers key, we replace the default with nothing by returning the NSNull, and finally for every other key we return nil, which will allow the default search pattern to continue.

If the delegate returns nil, then the next place the layer looks for the animation is in the actions dictionary. This property is nil by default, so if you do nothing, the search will continue. However, we can place an animation into the actions dictionary, and that one will be used instead of the default. Here is the code to replace the default opacity animation using the actions dictionary:

```
- (void)setUpAnimations:(CALayer *)layer {
  CABasicAnimation *animation = [CABasicAnimation animation];
  animation.duration = 0.5f;
  layer.actions = [NSDictionary dictionaryWithObject:animation
                                              forKey:@"opacity"];
}
```

The styles dictionary is searched next. If the styles dictionary is not nil, it is asked for the value for the actions key. If that is not nil and an animation is found for the key there, then it's returned and run. To use this approach in the earlier setUpAnimation:, we'd create a dictionary to hold the opacity animation as before, but we'd create a second dictionary as well and place the first under the animations key. This second dictionary would then become the style dictionary.

And finally, if none of the previous checks returns NSNull or a valid animation, then the layer's own defaultActionForKey: method is invoked. This final method invocation is where all the default implied animations come from.

This chapter has covered a lot of ground, but we have finally made our transition to fully layer-based animations. You can build full user interfaces based on your knowledge of layers now. Let's return to our discussion of the other new and unique features of layers by discussing scrolling and geometry.

The greater the difficulty, the more the glory in surmounting it.

▶ Epicurus

Chapter 9

Layer Scrolling and Geometry

Scrolling a layer is similar to scrolling a view in AppKit. The few differences that exist are on the API level, so you should have no trouble picking it up very quickly. The first part of this chapter is all about scrolling, and we cover an example in depth. Later in the chapter we look at how to take advantage of the various aspects of the geometry of layers to get just the look we want.

9.1 Scrolling Layers

Scrolling allows us to capture more than will fit in the screen at any one time and arrange that into a metaphor that our users understand. We are all familiar with the scroll bars that are used throughout Mac OS X in applications such as TextEdit. They allow us to see the size of our documents at a glance (the smaller the scroll knob, the bigger the document). But most important, they let us navigate to parts of the document that are not visible. The real document seems to extend above and below the window, and the scroller lets us move that document up and down so that we can see the whole document in parts that fit on our screens.

Core Animation provides CAScrollLayer to make it easier for us to scroll layer-based content. Conceptually, scrolling in Core Animation works the same way as in AppKit. The scroll layer performs the tasks of the "clipping view" from AppKit and is placed over a "too large to show" layer (the document layer if you will), and as the scroller's bounds rectangle is moved, different parts of the underlying layer are visible. The CAScrollLayer clips its sublayers, which is different from the other layer

AppKit Scrolling

Technically the way that scrolling works in AppKit is that the document view displays a document (*document* is a loose term here; it could be text and an image or a custom drawing that we do in our applications) that is too big to fit within the UI space allotted to it. Then a *clipping* view is placed over this document view. As the name implies, the clipping view clips the document view to the appropriate viewable space on the UI. The clipping view's frame remains constant (that is, it does not move on the UI), but its bounds change. As the clip view's bounds change, different parts of the underlying document view are exposed. Then over the top of the clipping and document view are placed the scroll bars and other UI treatments.

types but consistent with its role. We will discuss clipping and layers in the next section in detail. For now just keep in mind that the sublayers of CAScrollLayer are clipped to the bounds of CAScrollLayer.

In the menu that we started developing in Chapter 7, *Core Animation*, on page 77, we have not needed a scrolling layer because we have not had too much content to show at once. However, conceptually the menu might grow to become quite large. We should be using a scroll layer so that we can accommodate as many menu items as necessary. In Figure 9.1, on the facing page, we can see the layer tree for the new setup (we will look at the code shortly).

The scroll layer will provide a place for the potentially too large to show menu layer to reside so that it can be clipped and shown in pieces that fit on the screen. In Figure 9.2, on the next page, we see conceptually what this layer tree would look like onscreen.

The root layer is hosted in the view, and scroll is a sublayer and hosts the menu layer. The scroll layer is then used to clip the menu layer and navigate around the menu. As the selected menu item moves below Option 5, the scroll's bounds is modified so that it shows Option 2 to Option 6, and so on, over the whole menu layer. But enough abstraction. Let's get into the code.

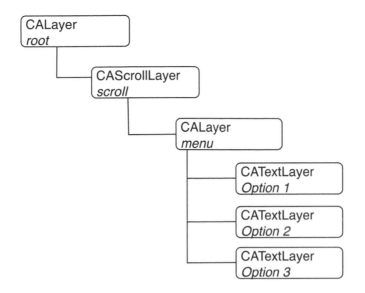

Figure 9.1: SCROLLING LAYER TREE

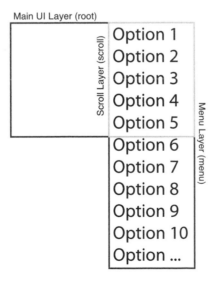

Figure 9.2: SCROLLING LAYER LAYOUT

LayerScrollingAndGeometry/SimpleMenuScrolling/MyControllerScroller.m

```
Line 1   - (void)awakeFromNib {
    -        self.offset = 10.0f;
    -        CALayer *layer = [CALayer layer];
    -        layer.name = @"root";
    5        layer.backgroundColor = [self black];
    -        layer.layoutManager = [CAConstraintLayoutManager layoutManager];
    -        [view setLayer:layer];
    -        [view setWantsLayer:YES];
    -        [view.layer addSublayer:[self scrollLayer]];
    10           [[view window] makeFirstResponder:view];
    -        [self performSelectorOnMainThread:@selector(selectItemAt:)
    -                                withObject:[NSNumber numberWithInteger:0]
    -                             waitUntilDone:NO];
    -    }
```

On line 1 in method awakeFromNib, the setup and configuration is more or less like we have seen before. The exception is that on line 9 we are adding the scrolling layer instead of the menu layer as a sublayer of root. And on the next line we are preparing to handle events by making our host view the firstResponder and then setting the selected item with a delayed perform of the selectItemAt: method. We will look at the particulars of event handling shortly, but for now note that we performed the selection method in a delayed fashion. This is required because the selection code relies on the layers being set up via their layout managers. As we discussed earlier, the layout manager will not be invoked until the next pass through the event loop, and since our selection code relies on the layout being done, we have to delay the invocation.

LayerScrollingAndGeometry/SimpleMenuScrolling/MyControllerScroller.m

```
Line 1   - (CAScrollLayer *)scrollLayer {
    -        CAScrollLayer *scrollLayer = [CAScrollLayer layer];
    -        scrollLayer.name = @"scroll";
    -        scrollLayer.layoutManager = [CAConstraintLayoutManager layoutManager];
    5        [scrollLayer addConstraint:
    -         [CAConstraint constraintWithAttribute:kCAConstraintMinX
    -                                    relativeTo:@"superlayer"
    -                                     attribute:kCAConstraintMidX
    -                                        offset:self.offset]];
    10       [scrollLayer addConstraint:
    -         [CAConstraint constraintWithAttribute:kCAConstraintMaxX
    -                                    relativeTo:@"superlayer"
    -                                     attribute:kCAConstraintMaxX
    -                                        offset:-self.offset]];
    15       [scrollLayer addConstraint:
    -         [CAConstraint constraintWithAttribute:kCAConstraintMinY
    -                                    relativeTo:@"superlayer"
    -                                     attribute:kCAConstraintMinY
    -                                        offset:self.offset]];
```

```
20     [scrollLayer addConstraint:
 -      [CAConstraint constraintWithAttribute:kCAConstraintMaxY
 -                                 relativeTo:@"superlayer"
 -                                  attribute:kCAConstraintMaxY
 -                                     offset:-self.offset]];
25     [scrollLayer addSublayer:[self menuLayer]];
 -     return scrollLayer;
 -   }
```

Next we create the scroll layer in the scrollLayer method on line 1. This
code is similar to the way we set up the menu layer in the previous
example. We constrain the scroll layer to be the same height and half the
width. At the end of this method, we add the menu layer as a sublayer.
Recall that this menu is going to be clipped to the bounds of the scroll
layer, and as the scroll layer's bounds rectangle is changed, different
parts of this layer will be displayed.

> LayerScrollingAndGeometry/SimpleMenuScrolling/MyControllerScroller.m

```
Line 1  - (CALayer *)menuLayer {
 -     CALayer *menu = [CALayer layer];
 -     menu.name = @"menu";
 -     [menu addConstraint:
 5      [CAConstraint constraintWithAttribute:kCAConstraintWidth
 -                                 relativeTo:@"superlayer"
 -                                  attribute:kCAConstraintWidth]];
 -     [menu addConstraint:
 -      [CAConstraint constraintWithAttribute:kCAConstraintMidX
10                                  relativeTo:@"superlayer"
 -                                  attribute:kCAConstraintMidX]];

 -     menu.layoutManager = [CAConstraintLayoutManager layoutManager];
 -     NSArray *names = [NSArray arrayWithObjects:
15                       @"Option 1 ", @"Option 2", @"Option 3", @"Option 4",
 -                       @"Option 5", @"Option 6", @"Option 7", @"Option 8",
 -                       @"Option 9", @"Option 10", @"Option 11", nil];
 -     NSArray *items = [self menuItemsFromNames:names];
 -     CGFloat height = self.offset;
20     for(CALayer *itemLayer in items) {
 -       height += itemLayer.preferredFrameSize.height + self.offset;
 -     }
 -     [menu setValue:[NSNumber numberWithFloat:height]
 -         forKeyPath:@"frame.size.height"];
25     [menu setSublayers:items];
 -     return menu;
 -   }
```

The menu layer is created in the menuLayer method starting on line
1. Some points to notice here are in the constraints. The menu layer is
constrained only in the width axis. This is on purpose because the layer
must be large enough to hold each of its sublayers, and it can't know

how large to be based on one of its siblings or its superlayer (that is, you can't specify a constraint based on a sublayer). On line 19, we start the calculation of the height, which simply adds the preferred size of each menu item and the offset for each item. And finally, we set the value on line 24. Notice that we are using setValue:forKeyPath:. Layers allow for their structure-based attributes (frame, bounds, position, transformation, and so on) to be set via setValue:forKeyPath:. Note, however, that the . notation of Objective-C 2.0 will not work for structure members (that is, we could not use layer.frame.size.height = 14.0f to set the height to 14.0f).

Now let's take a look at the code that manages the selected menu item. Here it is:

LayerScrollingAndGeometry/SimpleMenuScrolling/MyControllerScroller.m

```
Line 1   - (void)selectItemAt:(NSNumber *)index {
    -        CAScrollLayer *scrollLayer = [[view.layer sublayers] objectAtIndex:0];
    -        CALayer *menuLayer = [[scrollLayer sublayers] objectAtIndex:0];
    -        NSInteger value = [index intValue];
    5        if(value < 0) {
    -            value = [[menuLayer sublayers] count] - 1;
    -        } else if (value >= [[menuLayer sublayers] count]) {
    -            value = 0;
    -        }
   10        [scrollLayer setValue:[NSNumber numberWithInteger:value]
    -                        forKey:@"selectedItem"];
    -        CALayer *itemLayer = [[menuLayer sublayers] objectAtIndex:value];
    -        [itemLayer scrollRectToVisible:itemLayer.bounds];
    -    }
   15
    -    - (void)selectNext {
    -        CAScrollLayer *scrollLayer = [[view.layer sublayers] objectAtIndex:0];
    -        NSNumber *selectedIndex = [scrollLayer valueForKey:@"selectedItem"];
    -        [self selectItemAt:
   20            [NSNumber numberWithInteger:[selectedIndex intValue] + 1]];
    -    }
    -
    -    - (void)selectPrevious {
    -        CAScrollLayer *scrollLayer = [[view.layer sublayers] objectAtIndex:0];
   25        NSNumber *selectedIndex = [scrollLayer valueForKey:@"selectedItem"];
    -        [self selectItemAt:
    -            [NSNumber numberWithInteger:[selectedIndex intValue] - 1]];
    -    }
```

The code is fairly straightforward, but there are two things we should talk about in detail. The first is on line 11, where we are using set-Value:forKey: for a key that otherwise does not exist on the layer. The layer class has extended key-value coding to allow us to attach just about any property we need or want to the layer. Of course, this can be abused, and we could end up with "kitchen sink" layers (layers with all sorts of unrelated information attached to them), but when used correctly, this feature is very useful. For example, consider if we were to write our own layout manager (which we will do later in this chapter); we could attach information to our layers that give hints to the layout manager about how the layer should be handled.

Finally, also notice that the selection is circular. When the user is on the last item and hits the Next button, they are taken to the first item. We are not yet applying any visual selection effects to our menu items. We will be doing that in the next section as we discuss the various aspects and properties of layers and discuss how we can apply them as well as animate them.

And finally, let's take a quick look at how the events make it to the controller in the first place. As with most event capture in Cocoa, we subclass NSView and override some methods to get notification when events happen. In our case, we want to know when the down arrow or up arrow keys are pressed on the keyboard. Here is the code:

`LayerScrollingAndGeometry/SimpleMenuScrolling/MyView.m`

```
-(void)moveUp:(id)sender {
  [controller selectPrevious];
}

-(void)moveDown:(id)sender {
  [controller selectNext];
}
```

In this case, we have simply overridden the moveDown: and moveUp: methods. Cocoa will receive the keyDown: events for us and turn them into moveUp: and moveDown: method calls on the first responder.

9.2 Geometry Properties

Understanding the geometry of a layer helps us understand a lot of how the layer mechanism works, so we will spend the next couple of pages going over these properties. Something to keep in mind, however, is that often we will be using constraints or a custom layout to manage the frame, bounds, and position of our layers. If you are using a layout manager, it will reset these properties on each layout operation, so you typically do not need to manually set them.

The origin of the default coordinate system for layers is in the bottom-left corner of the layer. The positive x-axis is to the right, the positive y-axis is pointing up to the top of the screen, and the positive z-axis is pointing out of the screen. The z-axis will become important as we discuss layers in three dimensions, but for now you can think of layers in two dimensions with the origin at the bottom left of the screen.

As you have already seen, layers live in a hierarchy, and to this point we have shown examples and discussed bits and pieces of how the geometry of the layers is used. In this section, we are going to get into the details of how the layer geometry works. The first property we will look at is the layer's frame rectangle.

Frame

The frame rectangle is in the superlayer's coordinate system, so setting the frame property positions the layer within its superlayer. The root layer's frame places it in the view that hosts it. In Figure 9.3, on the facing page, we see that the origin of the image1 layer is at (25,10), and the width and height are 40 and 40, respectively. So, in the root coordinate system, the image1 layer is square and two and a half times farther from the right edge than it is up from the bottom. It is important to note that these coordinates are in the coordinate system of the root layer because that coordinate system will affect how the image layer looks on the screen. For example, if the root layer were scaled by one half in the horizontal direction, then image1 would appear to be a rectangle that is half as wide as it is tall. We will talk more about scaling and such later in this section.

Another aspect of the frame to be aware of is that it is computed rather than stored. So when we set the frame, what we are really doing is setting two other properties, the bounds and the position. We will discuss bounds next and then position.

Bounds

The bounds rectangle defines the coordinate system that the sublayers will be placed into. Any content placed into a layer is positioned relative to the bounds of that layer. In many cases, the layer's bounds origin is set to (0,0), so the content is positioned as we would expect. That is, if the frame for a sublayer is set to (25,25), then the sublayer will appear 25 units from the left border and 25 units from the bottom border. In Figure 9.3, on the next page, the origin bounds of the root layer is (0, 0),

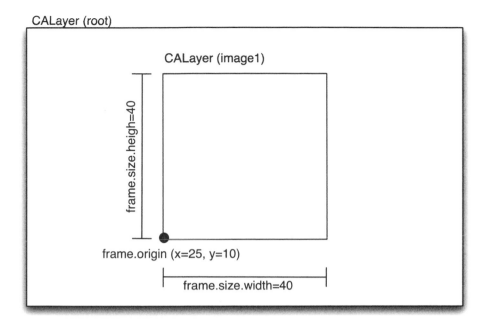

Figure 9.3: LAYER FRAME PROPERTY

so image1 appears 25 from the left border and 10 up from the bottom. Let's take a look at another case where the origin of the bounds is not set to (0,0).

In Figure 9.4, on the following page, the origin of the bounds is set to (10,0), and even though the frame of image1 is (25,10), it appears only 15 units from the left edge. This is because the bounds.origin of root is set to be 10 units to the left, so all sublayers in root appear to be 10 units left of what their values would lead us to believe they will appear. If you think back to our discussion of scrolling, this might seem familiar. A scrolling layer uses the translation properties of the bounds origin to move through the contents of its underlying layer. As the bounds of the scrolling layer is moved right or left and up or down, the underlying layers appear to be positioned differently. In fact, it's the scroll layer that is "moving" and the underlying document that is staying "still" within the coordinate system of its superlayer.

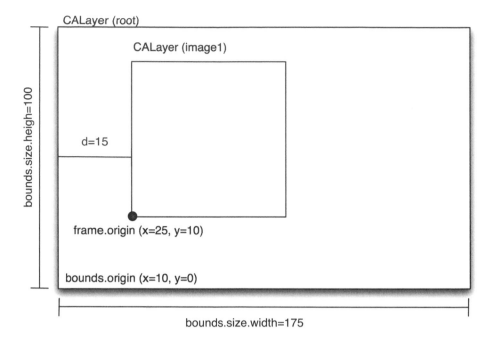

Figure 9.4: Layer bounds property

Position

The position specifies the location of a layer in its superlayer's coordinate system. The position is different from the frame.origin property because the position is based on the anchorPoint (which we will talk about next) instead of the lower-left corner of the layer. Basically, position allows us to generalize the way we position, scale, and rotate the layer. Any of the transformation operations act on the position rather than the lower-left corner (that is, the frame.origin). Let's look at the anchorPoint to get a better feel for what the position property is and how it works.

Anchor Point

The anchorPoint is the point around which all transformation and positioning manipulations take place. Another way to think of the anchor point is like a pin in the layer where its "attached" to its superlayer. As the layer is moved, the spot that moves is the anchor point, which is picked up and pushed back into the new spot. If the layer is rotated, it's around the anchor point, and if the layer is scaled, it's also around the anchor point.

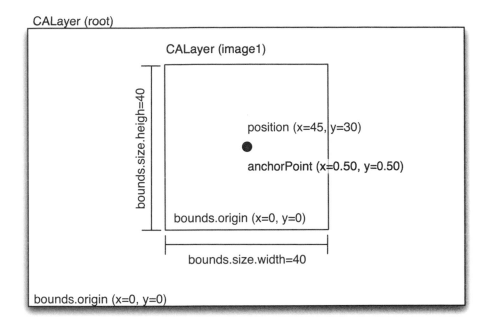

Figure 9.5: ANCHOR POINT DEFAULT LOCATION

The anchorPoint is *normalized*, meaning that its coordinates lie between 0.0 and 1.0, like a percentage. The default value for the anchor point is (0.5, 0.5), so it starts in the center of the layer. Looking at Figure 9.5, we see a visual of the default location of the anchor point.

This is the same layer we were looking at earlier in terms of its frame property. We have now changed to focusing on the bounds and position in this figure.

Recall that the position is the point in the superlayer where the anchorPoint is placed. As the anchorPoint is moved within the layer, the layer is repositioned within its superlayer. Let's look at some diagrams to try to make this a bit more concrete. The frame references in the following diagrams are specified as {{x, y}, {width, height}} in keeping with the CGRect struct.

In Figure 9.6, on the following page, we see the anchorPoint at its default location of (0.5, 0.5), so the frame of the image1 layer is {{25, 10}, {40, 40}}. In Figure 9.7, on page 127, we see the anchorPoint moved to {0.25, 0.5}. Note how the frame of image1 has changed. The origin of the frame has

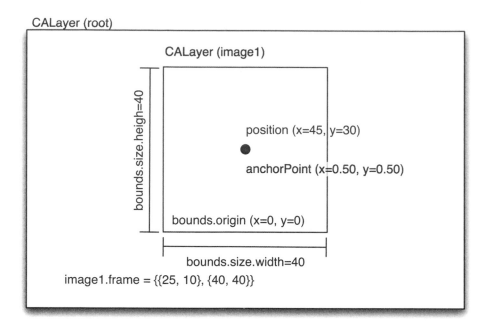

Figure 9.6: FRAME WITH ANCHOR POINT DEFAULT

moved from {25, 10} to {35, 10}. Since the frame width of the image1 layer is 40 and the anchorPoint moved 25% to the left, we multiply 0.25 by 40 (the move in the anchorPoint multiplied by the width) to get 10 units. The layer then visually moves to the right by 10 units because the position remained constant at {45, 30}.

The anchorPoint property takes some getting used to and a bit of tinkering with to get fully familiar with it. Spend a bit of time changing values in some test code (the code that comes with the book has an example app that lets you adjust the anchor point with a slider), and it will become clearer. In the meantime, though, don't worry too much about it because most of the time the anchorPoint is left at its default value in the center of the layer. Next let's talk about the cornerRadius property.

Corner Radius

The cornerRadius property allows us to specify the radius of the curvature of the corners of our layers. Rounded corners are not always needed, but they can provide a softening effect to the interface when used. If we set the layer to clip its contents, we can put a movie into

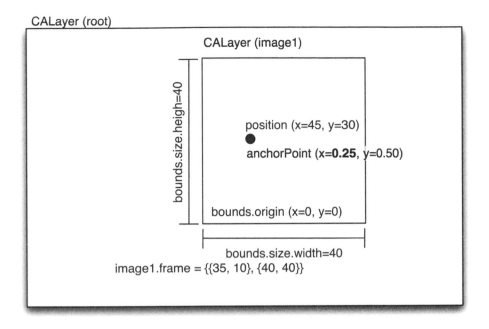

Figure 9.7: FRAME WITH ANCHOR POINT DEFAULT

a layer and have it play with rounded corners, but we are getting a bit ahead of ourselves. We will talk more about movies in layers in Chapter 11, *Media Layers*, on page 147.

Layer Depth

Each layer has an implicit or default depth into or out of the screen specified by the zPosition property. The default zPosition is zero. So when we add sublayers, each of them begins with a zPosition of zero and is displayed in the order of the sublayers array. If we change the zPosition, however, they will be ordered according to their depth. Layers with the smallest (or most negative) zPosition will be displayed first, and the layers with higher zPositions will be displayed last. The content is ordered first on zPosition, and then if a group of sublayers has the same zPosition, the sublayers are ordered according to their order in the sublayers array. We will look more at the nature of zPosition when we get into layers in 3D space.

Transformations

Transformations change a layer's look by applying matrix operations to the layer's geometry. A detailed discussion of the math behind matrix manipulation of coordinate systems is beyond this book, but we really don't need to know those details to use transformations. There are many different ways we can transform the geometry of a layer, but we will discuss only translation, scaling, and rotating in this section. We will discuss perspective transformations in the section on layers in 3D space.

Translation adds a constant to each component of each point in the coordinate system of the layer. Another way to think about it is that a translation simply moves the layer the specified amount along each of the axes. We can get a translation matrix with the CATransform3DMake-Translation function. This function takes three arguments, the amount to translate along each of the axes, and returns a CATransform3D struct that we can then assign to the transform property on our layer.

Scaling multiplies each of the components of each point in a layer by the specified factor. It has the effect of making things in the layer appear bigger (factors greater than 1) or smaller (factors less than 1 but greater than zero, negative factors flip the image). You get a scaling matrix via the CATransform3DMakeScale function. This also returns a CATransform3D that can be used as the transform value on any layer. The center of the scaling operation is the anchorPoint, so if you scale up by 2 along the x- and y-axes and the anchor point is in the center of the layer, then the edges will move an equal amount in each direction. If the anchor point has been moved, then the scaling will take place around that new location.

Rotation transformations rotate the layer around its anchor point. The rotation transformation is made via the CATransform3DMakeRotation function. The first argument is the amount to rotate in radians. The next three arguments define the vector around which the rotation is performed. Often we will be simply rotating around the z-axis (the axis pointing out of the screen and what we typically think about when we think about rotating shapes). To rotate 45 degrees around the z-axis, we would use the vector (0.0, 0.0, 1.0) with the angle (45.0 * π / 180.0).

A more detailed treatment of the math of 3D matrix math is beyond the scope of this book, but there are many resources on the Internet that go into great detail about 3D transformations including rotation.

9.3 Layers in 3D Space

It's important to keep in mind that layers live in a three-dimensional world. Each layer has not only the typical x and y coordinates but also the depth coordinate of z. As we perform various transformations on our layers, the transformations can be moved through this 3D space to achieve some stunning effects. In the next chapter, we will build on our Front Row–like example application, and we will see how we can apply this knowledge to get icons to move on a platter like they do on the left side of the screen in Front Row.

It has long been an axiom of mine that the little things are
infinitely the most important.
► Sir Arthur Conan Doyle

Chapter 10

Layers in 3D

In this chapter, we will look at three techniques we can use to make our layer-based user interfaces look more three-dimensional. First we will look at visual treatments that give the appearance of 3D to our UI elements. These tricks have long been used by digital artists to add depth to their creations. We will apply this technique to the selected menu item in our Front Row–like application so that it is clear to the user which layer is selected.

We will then place our objects into 3D space by using the zPosition property that is on every layer. We will be adding icons to the left of our UI to further emphasize what is selected. The icons will appear to move in 3D space around the outside of a platter.

In the final section, we will actually do the math to place our objects on the outer rim of a platter that sits in 3D space alongside our menu. In this section, we will cover the use of the CATransform3D and go into how to use it to achieve some really cool visual effects.

10.1 Adding Depth to Layer Appearance

In the overall Leopard UI, we see dramatic shadows to emphasize the active window. But in reality, apart from being drawn last, the window is not really "on top" of the other windows. It's just made to look that way. The same goes for many layer-based user interface treatments. Some of the tricks are different, but the idea remains that we make the elements look 3D by applying visual treatments.

Look at the Front Row UI. The selected menu item (Movies, TV Shows, and so on) is highlighted to look like it's 3D. We will be building out our Front Row–like application to gain some polish for the selected item to

Figure 10.1: MENU SELECTION HIGHLIGHTED

make it look more 3D. The goal of our work in this section will be to make our UI look like Figure 10.1.

As we can see, the selected item has several effects applied to it to make it stand out. First there is a shadow around it that makes it seem to come out of the screen, and second there is the slight white highlight at the top of the layer that looks like a reflection. Combined, these effects make the selected layer appear to be raised out of the screen. We are going to take our example that we left off with in Chapter 7, *Core Animation*, on page 77 and see how we can enhance it to add these effects.

As we left our example in the previous chapter, we had a scrolling layer over our menu items so that we could accommodate more than the items that could fit on the page. Now as we move into this stage of our UI development, the scrolling will become less important because we have only seven items to fit into the menu. So, you won't see much scrolling in this example, but all the code is still there and will still work if we end up with more than the items that fit.

Let's dig into the code and how this new 3D look is made. We saw in Section 5.3, *View Shadow*, on page 56 how to apply shadows (to views, but the same approach is used to apply them to layers). The only trick here is that we set the color of the shadow to blue instead of some shade of gray. Not that there is anything wrong with gray; it's just that blue looks cool.

The other effect that adds depth (and really makes the effect) is the reflection on the top half of the selection. This effect is achieved by adding a layer that masks to its bounds. Then add a sublayer to the masking layer that has its color set to white and its opacity set to 25%. Since the first layer masks its sublayers, the white layer will be invisible except for the part that is within the parent layer. Let's look at the code to make this a bit more concrete:

LayersIn3D/MenuLayout/MyControllerScroller.m

```
Line 1   highlightLayer = [CALayer layer];
    -    highlightLayer.masksToBounds = YES;
    -    highlightLayer.zPosition = -100.0f;
    -    highlightLayer.layoutManager = [CAConstraintLayoutManager layoutManager];
```

Here we are simply creating a layer and setting its layoutManager. The interesting bit that we apply to make the reflection look convincing is having the layer clip its sublayers on line 2. Also notice that we are setting the zPosition of the highlight layer. The zPosition determines what order the sublayers are drawn in (furthest back first). Having a value of -100.0 will make the highlightLayer be placed behind all the other sublayers that have a higher zPosition. Since the default is zero and we are not setting any other layer's zPosition, the highlight is placed behind the other sublayers (the arrow and text layers). Next up, let's look at how this layer is placed in its superlayer:

LayersIn3D/MenuLayout/MyControllerScroller.m

```
Line 1   [highlightLayer addConstraint:
    -      [CAConstraint constraintWithAttribute:kCAConstraintWidth
                                    relativeTo:@"superlayer"
                                     attribute:kCAConstraintWidth]];
    5    [highlightLayer addConstraint:
    -      [CAConstraint constraintWithAttribute:kCAConstraintHeight
                                    relativeTo:@"superlayer"
                                     attribute:kCAConstraintHeight]];
    -    [highlightLayer addConstraint:
   10      [CAConstraint constraintWithAttribute:kCAConstraintMinX
                                    relativeTo:@"superlayer"
                                     attribute:kCAConstraintMinX]];
    -    [highlightLayer addConstraint:
    -      [CAConstraint constraintWithAttribute:kCAConstraintMinY
   15                                   relativeTo:@"superlayer"
                                     attribute:kCAConstraintMinY]];
```

In this code, we are making sure that no matter which of the menu layers our highlightLayer is placed into, the highlight will always be the same width and height and have its origin set to the origin of the menu layer. In other words, this highlight layer is placed directly under and takes up all the space in the menu layer (since its zPosition is -100, it is drawn behind the text). Next up is creating the reflection:

LayersIn3D/MenuLayout/MyControllerScroller.m

```
Line 1  CALayer *reflectionLayer = [CALayer layer];
   -    reflectionLayer.backgroundColor = [self white];
   -    reflectionLayer.opacity = 0.25f;
   -    reflectionLayer.cornerRadius = 6.0f;
```

Here we are creating the layer that will become our reflection effect. We set the color to white on line 2 and then set the opacity to 25%. Since the layer is set to be translucent, it actually looks like a reflection. This is a critical part of the illusion. Finally, we set the radius of the corner to 6 to make it look like the edges of the selected layer are beveled in as well. Using a solid white color in the reflection layer works well enough for this example, but an even more convincing effect would be to use a gradient. Instead of setting the background color for this layer, we could draw a gradient (either through a delegate or by subclassing CALayer; see Chapter 8, *Core Animation Layers*, on page 93 for more details on drawing in layers). The gradient will add that extra bit of detail that will really make this effect look great. And finally we lay out the reflection layer in the highlight layer:

LayersIn3D/MenuLayout/MyControllerScroller.m

```
Line 1  [reflectionLayer addConstraint:
   -     [CAConstraint constraintWithAttribute:kCAConstraintWidth
   -                                 relativeTo:@"superlayer"
   -                                  attribute:kCAConstraintWidth]];
   5    [reflectionLayer addConstraint:
   -     [CAConstraint constraintWithAttribute:kCAConstraintHeight
   -                                 relativeTo:@"superlayer"
   -                                  attribute:kCAConstraintHeight]];
   -    [reflectionLayer addConstraint:
   10    [CAConstraint constraintWithAttribute:kCAConstraintMinX
   -                                 relativeTo:@"superlayer"
   -                                  attribute:kCAConstraintMinX]];
   -    [reflectionLayer addConstraint:
   -     [CAConstraint constraintWithAttribute:kCAConstraintMinY
   15                                relativeTo:@"superlayer"
   -                                  attribute:kCAConstraintMidY
   -                                     offset:self.offset/2.0f]];
   -    [highlightLayer addSublayer:reflectionLayer];
```

With these constraints, the reflectionLayer is always the same width and height as the highlightLayer, and its horizontal placement (the x origin) is the same as highlightLayer as well. However, its y origin is halfway up the highlightLayer plus a bit of an offset (on line 13). If the highlightLayer masks its sublayers, this white translucent layer is clipped. If the highlightLayer did not mask its sublayers, the reflectionLayer would be visible outside the highlightLayer and would not look like a reflection at all. I encourage you to mess with the example and turn off masking to see what this effect looks like in that case.

Now let's take a look at how the effects are applied to the selected layer:

LayersIn3D/MenuLayout/MyControllerScroller.m

```
itemLayer.shadowOpacity = 0.85f;
CALayer *highlight = [self highlightLayer];
[itemLayer addSublayer:highlight];
```

In these few lines of code, we are applying the effects to the selected menu layer. We are making sure the shadow is visible by setting its opacity to 85% and then adding the highlight layer. When another menu layer is selected, we simply have to remove the highlight layer from its superlayer and turn the shadow opacity back to 0%, and the effects will disappear.

Now that we have seen an example of making a layer appear to be 3D with subtle effects, let's dig into placing a layer into 3D space.

10.2 Custom Layer Layout

Now that we have the menu on the right side of our layer, it's time to get the images to float around on the platter on the left. We will make this happen by arranging (through a custom layout class) the icons in 3D space so they appear to be on the outer rim of a 3D platter. We will take two approaches to this so that you can gain some experience in the various approaches that are open to you with Core Animation in making 3D user interfaces. The first approach will be to use coordinates to approximate the images moving on a platter. The second approach will use 3D transformations, covered in Section 10.3, *3D Transformations*, on page 141.

NSKeyValueCoding Extensions

The layer and animation classes extend the NSKeyValueCoding protocol to add support for arbitrary keys. It is this support that allows us to add

Figure 10.2: ICONS ON PLATTER RIM

arbitrary attributes to CALayer and CAAnimation instances. It is typical to use this feature when building a custom layout. This support allows us to call setValue:forKey: on our layers for keys that don't exist on the layer. The layer will simply store the value under that key and return it when asked. We will make use of this feature shortly to keep track of info to make our custom layout easier to implement.

Before we get into the details of how to make this user interface, let's look at the screen shot in Figure 10.2.

On the right side, we see the same elements we had in the previous section: seven menu items that we can move between with the up and down arrow keys. On the right side we see a set of icons that are laid out on a platter that goes back into the screen. Each menu item selection change causes the platter to rotate and the front icon to change. Of course, on paper, the animation is a bit difficult to see, so fire up the app if you can and look at it for yourself.

The images used in this example are simple system images. They were chosen because they are on every Mac OS X Leopard distribution. Instead of confusing you by having to look for images in various places that you might have applications installed, it's simpler to just use these system images that are in well-defined places.

Let's look at the code we use to set it up. This code is extracted from the awakeFromNib method in our controller (the same controller from the previous example).

`LayersIn3D/Platter/MyController.m`

```
CALayer *platterLayer = [self platterLayer];
[view.layer addSublayer:platterLayer];
[view.layer setValue:platterLayer forKey:@"platterLayer"];
[self performSelectorOnMainThread:@selector(selectItemAt:)
                       withObject:[NSNumber numberWithInteger:0]
                    waitUntilDone:NO];
```

Here we are getting the platter layer and then adding it as a sublayer. We also set it under the key platterLayer (using the key-value coding extensions discussed earlier) so we can find it easily when the selection changes. Next up let's look at the code that creates and arranges the platter layer:

`LayersIn3D/Platter/MyController.m`

```
Line 1  - (CALayer *)platterLayer {
          CALayer *platterLayer = [CALayer layer];
          platterLayer.layoutManager = [PlatterLayoutManager layoutManager];
          NSArray *imageNames = [NSArray arrayWithObjects:NSImageNameBonjour,
5                        NSImageNameDotMac, NSImageNameComputer,
                         NSImageNameFolderBurnable, NSImageNameFolderSmart,
                         NSImageNameNetwork, NSImageNameColorPanel, nil];
          NSArray *imageLayers = [self platterImageLayersForImageNames:imageNames];
          platterLayer.sublayers = imageLayers;
10        [platterLayer addConstraint:
           [CAConstraint constraintWithAttribute:kCAConstraintMinX
                                      relativeTo:@"superlayer"
                                       attribute:kCAConstraintMinX]];
          [platterLayer addConstraint:
15         [CAConstraint constraintWithAttribute:kCAConstraintMaxX
                                      relativeTo:@"superlayer"
                                       attribute:kCAConstraintMidX]];
          [platterLayer addConstraint:
           [CAConstraint constraintWithAttribute:kCAConstraintMinY
20                                     relativeTo:@"superlayer"
                                       attribute:kCAConstraintMinY]];
          [platterLayer addConstraint:
           [CAConstraint constraintWithAttribute:kCAConstraintMaxY
                                      relativeTo:@"superlayer"
25                                     attribute:kCAConstraintMaxY]];
          return platterLayer;
        }
```

In this method we are creating and configuring the platter layer with constraints and sublayers. On line 8, we create the sublayers, and then on the next line we set the sublayers array. The next several lines of code arrange the platter layer in its superlayer. And finally, let's look at line 3. Here we are setting the layout manager for our platter layer to a custom layout manager. Let's look at the custom layout manager from the PlatterLayoutManager class. But before we do, we need to discuss the CALayoutManager informal protocol.

CALayoutManager invalidateLayoutOfLayer

This method is part of the CALayoutManager informal protocol. This protocol specifies methods that allow us to lay out the sublayers of a layer in any configuration we want. There are three methods in this protocol. The first is invalidateLayoutOfLayer:, which is called near the beginning of the layout cycle to give the manager a chance to get rid of any cached data. In this example we are not caching any information, so we don't need to implement this method.

CALayoutManager layoutSublayersOfLayer

The next method is where all the layout code goes. This method is responsible for placing each sublayer of the layer into its proper place. We have a lot of freedom in what we do with the sublayers of our layer in this method. We can set the sublayers wherever we want so that we get the look that we want. Here is the code for the layoutSublayersOfLayer: method:

LayersIn3D/Platter/PlatterLayoutManager.m

```
Line 1  - (void)layoutSublayersOfLayer:(CALayer *)layer {
   -        NSNumber *selectedItemIndex = [layer valueForKey:@"selectedItem"];
   -        NSInteger selectedItemIndexInt = [selectedItemIndex intValue];
   -        CALayer *selectedImageLayer = [[layer sublayers]
   5                                            objectAtIndex:selectedItemIndexInt];
   -        CGRect layerBounds = layer.bounds;
   -        CGPoint selectedPosition =
   -        CGPointMake(layerBounds.size.width - selectedImageSize / 1.5f,
   -                    layerBounds.size.height / 2.0);
  10        NSInteger index = 0;
   -        for(index = 0;index < [[layer sublayers] count];index++) {
   -          CALayer *sublayer = [[layer sublayers] objectAtIndex:index];
   -          if(sublayer == selectedImageLayer) {
   -            selectedImageLayer.zPosition = 100.0f;
  15            selectedImageLayer.bounds = CGRectMake(0.0f, 0.0f,
   -                                                    selectedImageSize,
   -                                                    selectedImageSize);
```

```
         selectedImageLayer.position = selectedPosition;
       } else {
20        NSInteger offset = selectedItemIndexInt - index;
         if(offset > 0) {
           sublayer.bounds = CGRectMake(0.0f, 0.0f, selectedImageSize * 2.0f,
                                        selectedImageSize * 2.0f);
           sublayer.position =
25         CGPointMake(-selectedImageSize * 2.0f,
                       selectedPosition.y + selectedImageSize/2.0f);
           sublayer.zPosition = 200.0f;
         } else {
           CGFloat unselectedImageSize =
30         selectedImageSize * (1.0f + (0.35f * offset));
           sublayer.bounds = CGRectMake(0.0f, 0.0f,
                                        unselectedImageSize,
                                        unselectedImageSize);
           sublayer.position =
35         CGPointMake(selectedPosition.x + (offset * 135.0f),
                       selectedPosition.y + (offset * 5.0f));
           sublayer.zPosition = offset * 30.0f;
         }
       }
40    }
    }
```

Remember that the goal of this method is to lay out all the image layers so they look like they are on the rim of a 3D platter. The images that are farther down in the sublayers array from the selection will be down and back from the selection. The farther down the list, the farther back and to the left. The images that are above the selected layer in the sublayers array will be pushed off the left side of the layer. The major steps required to perform this layout are as follows:

1. Find the selected image layer and its index in the sublayers array.

2. Iterate through the list of sublayers.

3. If you are on the selected layer, place it centered vertically and close to the right side of the layer.

4. If you are on a layer above the selected layer, then push it off the screen to the left, and make its size larger and zPosition higher.

5. if we are on a layer below the selected layer, make its zPosition less and its size smaller, and push it slightly to the left.

Starting on line 2, we get the index for the selected image layer and then get the selectedImageLayer from the layer's sublayers. Next on line 9, we calculate the position of the selected image. There is no magic in these numbers, so a good exercise would be to tweak these numbers and see how the layout changes.

Next we iterate through the sublayers starting on line 11. We first check to see whether we have hit the selected layer and, if so, set its position, zPosition, and bounds. If we are not on the selected layer, then we need to move the layer back and to the left or front and to the left. That is what we do next on line 19. If the offset is greater than zero, then we have a layer that is in front of the selected layer, so we need to move it off to the left and make its zPosition larger. We also make it bigger to enhance the illusion that it's moving toward the user.

And finally we position the layers that are behind the selected layer. We reduce its size by 35% for each step it is behind the selected layer and set its position to be below and to the left of the selection. Again, none of these numbers was specifically chosen for any other reason than they looked good to me. Please change them and experiment with what looks best to you.

CALayoutManager preferredSizeOfLayer

This method is called when the preferredFrameSize method is executed on the layer. The layout manager is responsible for calculating the preferred size of the layer and returning it. The preferred size depends on your goal in your layout. Some typical implementations for examples might be making the layer big enough to hold all its sublayers or making it big enough to hold the specified subset of its sublayers. There is no right answer on how to implement this method. This method is optional, so you don't have to implement it. If you don't, the default implementation returns the size of the layer's bounds rectangle.

Returning to the controller in our example, let's look now at how we change the selected image layer and then how we get the layout manager to lay out our images:

LayersIn3D/Platter/MyController.m

```
[platterLayer setValue:[NSNumber numberWithInteger:value]
               forKey:@"selectedItem"];
[platterLayer setNeedsLayout];
```

Here, we set the selected index via the key-value encoding method and then tell the layer it should be laid out by calling setNeedsLayout. Calling setNeedsLayout is somewhat like the setNeedsDisplay: on NSView that we are familiar with.

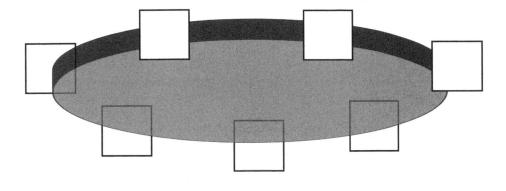

Figure 10.3: A SIMPLFIED 3D REPRESENTATION OF THE PLATTER AND ICONS

In this section, we have seen a layout manager that simulates the 3D platter effect. Although this looks great and works like a champ, sometimes we might need or want a more accurate 3D representation of the effect we are looking for. In the next section, we will use CATransform3Ds to place our layers into 3D space in a much more accurate way than we did with this simulation.

10.3 3D Transformations

Now that we have our 3D scene working, we want to change it so that our images are placed in a 3D space. In the previous example, we did a bit of 3D by setting the zPosition attribute. But we manually calculated that value (or just played with it until it looked good), and Core Animation is capable of true 3D placement of objects. There are cases where you'd want to use one of these techniques. If you are able to get the effect you want using manual placement, then by all means go with that approach; sometimes it can be simpler. But if you find yourself writing a bunch of code to try to make something look more 3D, then you should consider using a true 3D transformation because it could greatly simplify your code. So, let's look into using the transform property.

As in the previous example, the bulk of the work happens in the layout manager. In Figure 10.3, you can see a simplified version of the look we are hoping to achieve. The platter is rotated along the x-axis by a few degrees, and then the icons are placed along the outer rim of the platter in equal increments. The selected item is on the right side as in the previous example. As we change selection, the icons rotate around the platter.

Let's look at the code to make this effect happen. This code is a bit long, so here is the big picture of what is going on here:

1. Set up a translation to the center of the platter on line 10.

2. Set up a translation to move out from the center by the radius on line 13.

3. Set up the rotation around the x-axis on line 18.

4. Iterate through the sublayers.

5. Apply the translations and rotations to build a transform matrix.

6. Set the transformation matrix on the layer on line 34.

LayersIn3D/Platter3DTransform/Platter3DLayoutManager.m

```
Line 1   - (void)layoutSublayersOfLayer:(CALayer *)layer {
             CGFloat platterRadius = 600.0f;
             NSNumber *selectedItemIndex = [layer valueForKey:@"selectedItem"];
             NSInteger selectedItemIndexInt = [selectedItemIndex intValue];
      5
             CGFloat platterXCenter = (layer.bounds.size.width * 3.0f/4.0f) -
             platterRadius;
             CGFloat platterYCenter = layer.bounds.size.height / 2.0f;

     10      CATransform3D platterCenterTranslate =
             CATransform3DMakeTranslation(platterXCenter, platterYCenter, 0.0f);

             CATransform3D platterRadiusTranslate =
             CATransform3DMakeTranslation(platterRadius, 0.0f, 0.0f);
     15
             CGFloat xRotationAngle = 2.5f * M_PI/180.0f;

             CATransform3D xRotation =
             CATransform3DMakeRotation(xRotationAngle, 1.0f, 0.0f, 0.0f);
     20
             NSInteger index = 0;
             for(index = 0;index < [[layer sublayers] count];index++) {
               NSInteger offset = index - selectedItemIndexInt;
               CALayer *sublayer = [[layer sublayers] objectAtIndex:index];
     25        CGFloat angle = offset * 360.0f/7.0f  * M_PI/180.f;
               CATransform3D yRotation =
               CATransform3DMakeRotation(angle, 0.0f, 1.0f, 0.0f);
               CATransform3D intermediate =
               CATransform3DConcat(xRotation, platterCenterTranslate);
     30        intermediate = CATransform3DConcat(yRotation, intermediate);
```

```
-        intermediate = CATransform3DConcat(platterRadiusTranslate, intermediate);
-        CATransform3D minusYRotation =
-        CATransform3DMakeRotation(-angle, 0.0f, 1.0f, 0.0f);
-        sublayer.transform = CATransform3DConcat(minusYRotation, intermediate);
35   }

-    NSInteger forwardIndex = (selectedItemIndexInt + 6) % 7;
-    CALayer *forwardLayer = [[layer sublayers] objectAtIndex:forwardIndex];
-    CATransform3D scale = CATransform3DMakeScale(1.2f, 1.2f, 1.0f);
40   forwardLayer.transform = CATransform3DConcat(scale, forwardLayer.transform);

-    NSInteger backwardIndex = (selectedItemIndexInt + 1) % 7;
-    CALayer *backwardLayer = [[layer sublayers] objectAtIndex:backwardIndex];
-    scale = CATransform3DMakeScale(0.8f, 0.8f, 1.0f);
45   backwardLayer.transform = CATransform3DConcat(scale, backwardLayer.transform);
-  }
```

Let's look at the code for each of these steps in detail. First we are creating a few transformations that we will use later. The CATransform3D is a C struct that Core Animation uses to represent a 3D transformation. The math behind a 3D transformation is beyond the scope of this book, but we will briefly cover what each of these transformation matrixes is and how we use each of them. The first transform on line 10 is a simple translation. A translation allows us to place our layers in 3D space. This transformation says move to the point platterXCenter in the x dimension, platterYCenter in the y dimension, and 0.0 in the z dimension. The center of the platter is centered along the height of the layer and pushed just offscreen to the left of the edge of the layer.

The next transform translates our layers out to the edge of the platter by moving platterRadius units along the x dimension. This brings us to the point of how these transformation matrixes are combined. If we were to simply apply this translation to our layers, they would all end up in the same place. Instead, we rotate around the rim of the platter once we translate out to the rim. We will see how this is done shortly. Finally, on line 18, we create the rotation along the x-axis so that our platter is slightly tipped up.

We create these three transformation matrixes here because they do not change for each layer like the next couple that we will create do. These are simply reused in the iteration.

Now as we iterate through the list of sublayers, we need to place each layer at an equal distance along the rim of the platter with the selected layer again on the far right of our layer in the center. First we calculate the offset on line 23. This offset will be positive for the layers behind the selected layer, negative for the layers in front of the selected layer, and zero for the selected layer. On line 25, we calculate the angle around the rim of the platter where the layer should be placed. Since we have seven layers, we divide 360 (the number of degrees in a circle) by 7 to get the measure in degrees and then convert that value to radians (all the CA angle measures are in radians). Next we create the y-rotation transformation matrix. This transformation says that we should rotate the layer around the y-axis by the angle measure we calculated in the previous step.

Next up we create an intermediate transformation that is the beginning of our transformation matrix that will eventually place the layer in the correct spot. The CATransform3DConcat() function takes the second argument, multiplies it with the first, and returns the result. There are lots of ways to think about this matrix multiplication, and if you are familiar with OpenGL transformations, you likely already have a mental model in place. So if you already have a mental model, use yours. If not, feel free to adopt mine.

Eventually the transformation will be applied to a layer. Conceptually what the transformations do is move, rotate, and otherwise change the location and orientation of the layer in 3D space. As you can imagine, the order in which we apply these transformation is important. Imagine in the real world if you placed a block on the corner of your desk; if you move it 50 units forward and then rotated it 90 degrees, it would end up in a very different place than if you rotated it 90 degrees and then moved it 50 units forward. The same concept applies to the way we concatenate these transformations. The concatenation is like "adding" the two transformations together (the math is really a matrix multiplication, but conceptually it is like adding the effects). So, our first call to CATransform3DConcat() is moving to the center of the platter and then rotating around the x-axis. Next up we take the result of this concatenation and apply the y-rotation to the mix, and finally we take this result and apply the translation to the rim of the platter on line 31.

That was a mouthful. It can be quite confusing to make the translation matrix do what you want. However, with time and experience, your intuition will build, and it will become second-nature. The way I got my head wrapped around it was to spend some time playing with a rotation matrix and a translation matrix and then tweaking the values and the order to see what happened.

Figure 10.4: THE ICONS ON A 3D PLATTER

And at the end of the loop, we apply a transformation that "undoes" the y-axis translation. The reason I do this is to counter the skew introduced by the other transformations. Sometimes this is exactly what you want, sometimes not. In this case, I thought the effect looked much better without the skewing, so I reversed it with this translation. Feel free to change it around and see whether you agree.

And finally, after the loop, we apply a bit of perspective to the icons that are in front and back of the selected icon starting on line 37. We make the icon in the front appear larger by scaling it up by 20 percent and the icon in back smaller by scaling it down 20 percent. Since we see only three icons at a time, we don't need to apply the perspective transform to each icon.

Now let's take a look at the UI in action in Figure 10.4.

As you press the up and down arrows, the selection changes, and the icons move around the outside of the platter. The effects lose a bit of their look on paper, so make sure to take a look at the running example.

In this chapter, we have seen the transition into a 3D world with layers. As we discussed, there are several ways to approach making your

UI look 3D. We can provide visual illusions like the reflection on the selected menu item, and we can go so far as creating 3D transformation matrixes that Core Animation will use to place our layers into the 3D environment.

There is a lot of room to play and experiment in what we have done so far. Some things that would be good to add to give our users a clearer picture of what is happening in our Front Row–like app is to add some filters to the unselected layers to make them less emphasized. Another approach would be to add some more rotation to the layers that are in front of the selected layer so that they translate off the screen. There are countless ways to tweak the UI. Always keep in mind, though, that we want to give our users something that increases their ability to understand what our app is doing.

If you deliberately plan on being less than you are capable of being, then I warn you that you'll be unhappy for the rest of your life.

▶ Abraham Maslow

Chapter 11

Media Layers

Core Animation lets you mix all the media types common on the Mac in one window at the same time. Before Core Animation, actions such as placing some controls over a QuickTime movie were possible but really error prone and tedious; they required lots of code and testing to make sure they worked. Enter Core Animation, and all that goes away. We can now fairly easily mix various content types into the same window and even animate all that content at once with layers.

In this chapter, I will introduce the three media layer types and show how to use each of them. The first is QuickTime layers, which allow you to load any type of media that QuickTime understands (which is quite a lot). You can even have a layer that captures video from your iSight camera. The next layer type is the Quartz Composer composition layer, which loads and run Quartz Composer compositions. And finally, we will cover the OpenGL layer. Let's get started with QuickTime layers.

11.1 QuickTime Layers

QuickTime is essentially a group of APIs and file formats that allow you to capture, create, and play back almost any type of media you can imagine.

QTKit is the Objective-C framework for accessing QuickTime. QTKit gives us two integration points for Core Animation. The QTMovieLayer allows QuickTime media played in a layer. The QTCaptureLayer allows us to place content from a capture device (such as your iSight camera) into a layer. The really cool thing is that you can use all the animation that you learned so far to animate your QuickTime content once you get that content into a layer.

Figure 11.1: MOVIE LAYERS IN ACTION

QuickTime is the basis of the media-playing functionality in iTunes, iMovie, Apple's Pro tools (Final Cut Studio), and thousands of other tools for content creation. Another great thing about QuickTime is that it's compatible with lots of consumer-level technologies such as the video cameras built into digital cameras. In fact, when you capture a video with your camera and load it into iPhoto, its playback is done via QuickTime. So if you are looking for a way to integrate your users' multimedia content into your application, QuickTime is the way to go. As you might expect, QuickTime is a huge topic worthy of a book on its own, so I won't be covering the QuickTime API in any detail other than what is needed for our examples.

Movie Layers

Movie layers allow us to show any content that QuickTime can load into a layer. That means you can load movies from URLs, your users' iPhoto libraries, the content from their Movies directories, or just about anywhere that QuickTime content can be found. In our example here, we will use the movies that you can use as backgrounds in iChat (via the Effects panel in a video chat). The movies are loaded into QTMovieLayer objects and then arranged via a layout manager. As you press the arrow keys, the selection changes, and the active playing movie changes. You can see a screen shot of the application in action in Figure 11.1.

As you can see from the screen shot, the inactive movies are blurred and scaled down, while the frontmost movie is not. As you switch movies, the current movie stops playing, and the newly selected movie starts.

The code starts in awakeFromNib, and apart from the typical setup code (making a layer, and so on), the movie layer is loaded via the loadMovieLayers on line 5, and the selected layer is set on line 6. Setting the selection is taking advantage of the key-value coding extensions, and the selected value is used by the MovieLayoutManager so it knows which layer to place front and center. Then the selected movie is played on line 8 by calling the playSelectedMovie (which we will look at shortly).

MediaLayers/MovieLayer/MovieLayerView.m

```
Line 1  - (void)awakeFromNib {
   -        self.layer = [CALayer layer];
   -        self.layer.backgroundColor = CGColorGetConstantColor(kCGColorBlack);
   -        [self setWantsLayer:YES];
   5        [self loadMovieLayers];
   -        [self.layer setValue:[NSNumber numberWithInt:0] forKey:@"selectedIndex"];
   -        self.layer.layoutManager = [MovieLayoutManager layoutManager];
   -        [self playSelectedMovie];
   -        [self becomeFirstResponder];
   10   }
```

The loadMovieLayers is responsible for loading the movies and then calling movieLayerWithMovie:named:, which creates the layers and associates the movies with them.

MediaLayers/MovieLayer/MovieLayerView.m

```
Line 1  - (void)loadMovieLayers {
   -        NSError *error = nil;
   -        NSString *path = @"/System/Library/Compositions";
   -        NSArray *movieNames = [[NSFileManager defaultManager]
   5                                  contentsOfDirectoryAtPath:path
   -                                  error:&error];
   -        for(NSString *movieName in movieNames) {
   -          if(![[movieName pathExtension] isEqualToString:@"mov"]) {
   -            continue;
   10         }
   -          NSString *moviePath = [path stringByAppendingPathComponent:movieName];
   -          if([QTMovie canInitWithFile:moviePath]) {
   -            NSError *error = nil;
   -            QTMovie *movie = [QTMovie movieWithFile:moviePath error:&error];
   15           if(nil == error) {
   -              CALayer *movieLayer = [self movieLayerWithMovie:movie named:movieName];
   -              [self.layer addSublayer:movieLayer];
   -            } else {
   -              NSLog(@"error = %@", error);
   20           }
   -          }
   -        }
   -      }
```

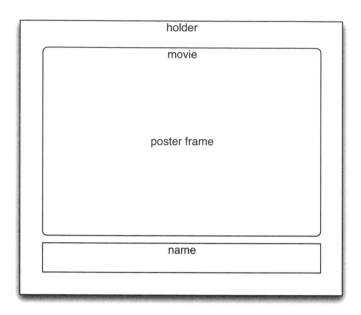

Figure 11.2: MOVIE LAYERS IN ACTION

On line 8, the code is making sure that only the .mov files are loaded from the composition directory. This has to be done for this example, because QuickTime will actually load Quartz Composer compositions that are in that directory, and since we are not quite ready for that, they are filtered out. The movie is then created starting on line 12 and ending with 14. It's important to check the error that QTMovie returns to make sure you have a valid movie. And finally, if there is a valid movie, a layer is created to hold that movie, and it's added to the view's layer. The movieLayerWithMovie:named: method is responsible for creating the movie layer.

The movie layer is actually several layers contained in one. In Figure 11.2, we can see the various layers and where they sit. The holder layer holds the movie and its title layer as well as the poster frame layer. We need the poster frame because as movie layers are created, they do not show any part of the movie until it is played. Since we want the layer to look like the movie, we grab posterImage from the movie and place that over the movie layer until we start playing the movie. As we start to play the movie, we set the hidden property of the poster layer to YES so that it fades away and shows the movie.

Here is the code to create the movie layer from the movieLayerWith-
Movie:named: method. The QTMovieLayer is created with the movie that
it will be displaying on line 1. Now that we have a layer, we can do
all the tricks we have learned so far. This movie layer can be rotated,
scaled, made transparent, and moved all in a beautifully animated way
just like the CALayers we have been animating. We can do some fairly
sophisticated things with this kind of functionality. You could implement a television-type interface that allows you to switch channels with
beautiful transitions instead of flashes. The possibilities are endless.
Another really cool thing is that this is just a layer like any other layer.
This layer can be placed on a user interface along with views and other
layers (more on this later).

MediaLayers/MovieLayer/MovieLayerView.m

```
Line 1   QTMovieLayer *movieLayer = [QTMovieLayer layerWithMovie:movie];
    -    movieLayer.name = [NSString stringWithFormat:@"movie - %@", movieName];
    -    movieLayer.cornerRadius = 14.0f;
    -    movieLayer.masksToBounds = YES;
    5    [movieLayer addConstraint:
    -     [CAConstraint constraintWithAttribute:kCAConstraintMidX
                                         relativeTo:@"superlayer"
                                          attribute:kCAConstraintMidX]];
    -    [movieLayer addConstraint:
   10     [CAConstraint constraintWithAttribute:kCAConstraintMaxY
                                         relativeTo:@"superlayer"
                                          attribute:kCAConstraintMaxY
                                             offset:-5.0f]];
```

The rest of the movieLayerWithMovie:named: method simply creates the
rest of the holder layer hierarchy and configures it properly. We have
seen code like this several times before, so let's go on to more Quick-
Time layer-related code.

The playSelectedMovie method is called at the end of awakeFromNib to
start playing the currently selected movie. Here is the code for that
method:

MediaLayers/MovieLayer/MovieLayerView.m

```
- (void)playSelectedMovie {
  NSInteger selection = [[self.layer valueForKey:@"selectedIndex"] intValue];
  CALayer *holderLayer = [self.layer.sublayers objectAtIndex:selection];
  QTMovie *movie = [holderLayer valueForKey:@"movie"];
  [movie play];
  [[holderLayer valueForKey:@"moviePosterLayer"] setHidden:YES];
}
```

Here the selected index is retrieved from the layer via the key selectedIn-dex and then used to get at the correct layer. The layer has the movie tag tied to the QTMovie that was placed there in movieLayerWithMovie:named:. After telling the movie to start playing, the moviePosterLayer is set to hidden so that we can see the movie instead of the poster image. The movies need to be stopped when they are no longer front and center using the stopSelectedMovie method.

MediaLayers/MovieLayer/MovieLayerView.m

```
- (void)stopSelectedMovie {
    NSInteger selection = [[self.layer valueForKey:@"selectedIndex"] intValue];
    CALayer *holderLayer = [self.layer.sublayers objectAtIndex:selection];
    QTMovie *movie = [holderLayer valueForKey:@"movie"];
    [movie stop];
}
```

This code is more or less the same as playSelectedMovie except that we are stopping the movie here and we don't have to do anything with the posterImage. As the right or up arrow keys are pressed, the selected index increases, and as the down or left arrow is pressed, the selected index decreases.

Now that we have seen how to start and stop the movie, let's look at the code to move to the next and previous movies. The selection is changed simply by setting a new value for the key selectedIndex and then calling setNeedsLayout on the layer. The layout manager will then take care of moving all the layers into their correct positions. Here is the code:

MediaLayers/MovieLayer/MovieLayerView.m

```
Line 1  - (void)moveUp:(id)sender {
            if([[NSApp currentEvent] modifierFlags] & NSShiftKeyMask) {
                [self.layer.layoutManager
                    setValue:[NSNumber numberWithBool:YES] forKey:@"slowMoFlag"];
        5   }
            [self moveToNextMovie];
        }

        - (void)moveToNextMovie {
        10  [self stopSelectedMovie];
            NSInteger selection = [[self.layer valueForKey:@"selectedIndex"] intValue];
            NSNumber *newSelection =
            [NSNumber numberWithInt:(selection + 1) % [self.layer.sublayers count]];
            [self.layer setValue:newSelection forKey:@"selectedIndex"];
        15  [self.layer setNeedsLayout];
            [self playSelectedMovie];
        }
```

Figure 11.3: Capture layer in action

In the moveUp: method, we are checking to see whether the Shift key is down and, if so, turning on slow-motion for the animation and then calling the moveToNextMovie method to update the selection and invoke the layout.

In moveToNextMovie on line 10, we are stopping the currently selected movie. Then we update the selection and tell the layer it needs to have its layout happen. Then on line 16, we start playing the currently selected movie by calling playSelectedMovie.

Now let's go on to the capture layer and see how we can mimic (in a very limited way) some of the functionality of Photo Booth and/or iChat video conferencing.

Capture Layers

Capture layers allow you to capture video and display that in a layer. Once in the layer, you can apply any sort of Core Animation tricks to it that you want. In the example here (shown in Figure 11.3), we will set up a capture session with your built-in iSight (or other connected, supported webcam) and turn a filter off and on. Let's get started.

The UI is simple; it merely plays back whatever the iSight is pointed at. As you click the image, a CIBloomFilter will selectively be placed over the image and will turn off as you click it again. If you run the application, you will also notice that the filter is animated.

Showing the video captured from a device in a layer involves five relatively easy steps:

1. Creating a new QTCaptureSession
2. Attaching to and opening a device via the QTCaptureDevice class
3. Creating a new input via the QTCaptureDeviceInput class
4. Adding the new device to the input
5. Adding the new input to the new session

The bulk of this process is in the captureSession method shown here:

MediaLayers/CaptureLayer/CaptureView.m

```objc
- (QTCaptureSession *)captureSession {
  static QTCaptureSession *session = nil;
  if(nil == session) {
    NSError *error = nil;
    session = [[QTCaptureSession alloc] init];
    // Find a video device
    QTCaptureDevice *device =
    [QTCaptureDevice defaultInputDeviceWithMediaType:QTMediaTypeVideo];
    if (device == nil) {
      NSLog (@"trying for a muxed device for video");
      device = [QTCaptureDevice
                  defaultInputDeviceWithMediaType:QTMediaTypeMuxed];
      if (device != nil)
        NSLog (@"got a muxed device for video");
    }
    // still no device?  time to bail
    if (device == nil) {
      error = [[[NSError alloc] initWithDomain:NSCocoaErrorDomain
                                     code:QTErrorDeviceNotConnected
                                 userInfo:nil] autorelease];
      [[NSAlert alertWithError:error] runModal];
      return nil;
    }
    [device open:&error];
    if(nil != error) {
      [[NSAlert alertWithError:error] runModal];
      return nil;
    }
    // Add a device input for that device to the capture session
    QTCaptureDeviceInput *input =
    [[QTCaptureDeviceInput alloc] initWithDevice:device];
    [session addInput:input error:&error];
    if(nil != error) {
      [[NSAlert alertWithError:error] runModal];
      return nil;
    }
  }
  return session;
}
```

In this code, we create a default session. Then we grab the default video device, create an input object for that default device, and add that input to the session. This is a really brief rundown of how the capturing of video is done via QTKit.

QTKit can find all connected input devices and give you a list that can be presented to your users. Then instead of choosing the default, you could grab the one the user selected. As I said earlier, there is a whole book waiting to be written on QuickTime, so I can't hope to cover it in any detail here; this should give you enough to get started on your own capture application.

Next we create the layer with this capture session so it can be added to our UI:

`MediaLayers/CaptureLayer/CaptureView.m`

```
Line 1   - (QTCaptureLayer *)captureLayer {
             if(nil == captureLayer) {
                 captureLayer = [QTCaptureLayer layerWithSession:self.captureSession];
                 captureLayer.cornerRadius = 16.0f;
      5          captureLayer.masksToBounds = YES;
                 captureLayer.bounds = CGRectMake(0.0f, 0.0f, 640.0f, 480.0f);
                 [captureLayer addConstraint:
                   [CAConstraint constraintWithAttribute:kCAConstraintMidX
                                            relativeTo:@"superlayer"
     10                                       attribute:kCAConstraintMidX]];
                 [captureLayer addConstraint:
                   [CAConstraint constraintWithAttribute:kCAConstraintMidY
                                            relativeTo:@"superlayer"
                                              attribute:kCAConstraintMidY]];
     15          [self.layer addSublayer:captureLayer];
                 [captureLayer.session startRunning];
             }
             return captureLayer;
         }
```

Notice on line 3 that the capture session created in the captureSession is used in the creation of the layer. Now there is a layer ready to be added to our UI. However, we do a bit of configuration to the layer to make it look just so, including adding a few constraints to make the layer show up in the center of the scene. Notice also that on line 16 the capture session is started. That line is what causes the QTKit machinery to connect to your webcam and start capturing content, so if you forget this line, you'll just get a nice black layer.

Finally, let's look at the code to turn off and on the animated Bloom filter. When you click the image, you toggle the filter.

Here is the code to make that happen:

MediaLayers/CaptureLayer/CaptureView.m

```
- (void)mouseDown:(NSEvent *)event {
  if(self.captureLayer.filters == nil) {
    self.captureLayer.filters = [NSArray arrayWithObject:self.filter];
    [self.captureLayer addAnimation:self.animation
     forKey:@"animateTheFilter"];
  } else {
    [self.captureLayer removeAnimationForKey:@"animateTheFilter"];
    self.captureLayer.filters = nil;
  }
}
```

Notice that we are simply adding the animation to the layer via addAnimation:forKey:. When the animation is added, it will start running immediately. Here is the code that creates the animation:

MediaLayers/CaptureLayer/CaptureView.m

```
- (CABasicAnimation *)animation {
  if(nil == animation) {
    NSString *keyPath = [NSString stringWithFormat:
                        @"filters.captureFilter.%@", kCIInputRadiusKey];
    animation = [CABasicAnimation animationWithKeyPath:keyPath];
    animation.repeatCount = 1.0e100f;
    animation.duration = 2.0f;
    animation.fromValue = [NSNumber numberWithFloat:1.0f];
    animation.toValue = [NSNumber numberWithFloat:15.0f];
    animation.autoreverses = YES;
  }
  return animation;
}
```

This is a straightforward animation that changes the value of the kCIInputRadiusKey between 1 and 15 and repeats virtually forever with a duration of two seconds per cycle.

Using this QTCaptureLayer, you can imagine a whole host of application that would be really fun to build and use. iChat's video chat functionality, Photo Booth's effects...that kind of functionality is now not only possible to add to your application but is relatively easy to do.

11.2 Quartz Composer Composition Layers

Back in Section 7.1, *Layer-Hosting Views*, on page 78, we saw our first taste of what a Quartz Composer composition might look like in our applications. In this section, I will show how to load a composition into a layer and animate the input values for the composition.

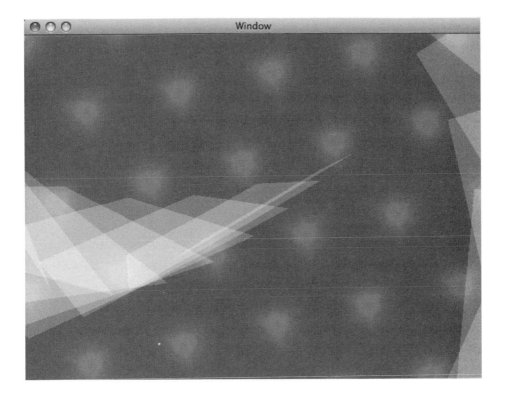

Figure 11.4: QUARTZ COMPOSER LAYER IN ACTION

Quartz Composer is a visual development tool that allows graphics designers and software developers to make animated graphics. The tool has a visual programming environment that makes it easy for nonprogrammers to use and make beautiful designs, but it also has some powerful capabilities that allow developers to control the compositions programmatically. Quartz Composer is another one of those topics that warrants a whole book to itself, so I won't have space to cover it in any detail. However, the composition that is used in this example will give you a feel for at least part of what is possible with Quartz Composer. In Figure 11.4, we see the app we are about to go over.

This layer shows the composition located at /Developer/Examples/Quartz Composer/Compositions/Graphic Animations/Cells.qtz. If you run the application, you can click the layer, and the speed of the stuff flying around on the screen changes from 0.25 to 3 times its normal speed. We will look at the code in just a second, but if you have run either the composition or the application, you might be thinking something like "Why in the world would I write code when I can do all this cool animation with Quartz Composer?" Well, Quartz Composer compositions are great for a lot of things, but you have much less control over how the elements in a composition act than you would over your own layers. So, use Quartz Composer for what it's good for (creating autonomous animations), and then integrate your creations into your application using layers. I think you will find that it's hard to stop playing with Quartz Composer once you get started, so spend some time getting to know this tool.

Now on to the code of how to integrate Quartz Composer compositions into your application:

MediaLayers/QuartzComposerLayers/QuartzCompositionView.m

```
- (QCCompositionLayer *)compositionLayer {
    return [QCCompositionLayer compositionLayerWithFile:[self compositionPath]];
}
```

This is the amazing part. We can take all the really cool compositions that ship with Leopard and use them in our applications with this one simple line of code. Another cool thing about using these compositions is that any changes made to them via a layer will result in an implicit animation (for any property of a type that can be animated). The Cells composition that we are using in this example has an exposed input property for the pace of the animation. We can change that value, and the speed of the composition will gradually change from where it is to the value we set it to. However, we can also animate this value with a key path and a basic animation. Let's look at that code here:

MediaLayers/QuartzComposerLayers/QuartzCompositionView.m

```
Line 1  - (CABasicAnimation *)animation {
     -      static CABasicAnimation *animation = nil;
     -      if(nil == animation) {
     -          NSString *keyPath = [NSString stringWithFormat:@"patch.%@.value",
     5                               QCCompositionInputPaceKey];
     -          animation = [CABasicAnimation animationWithKeyPath:keyPath];
     -          animation.repeatCount = 1.0e100;
     -          animation.fromValue = [NSNumber numberWithFloat:0.25f];
     -          animation.toValue = [NSNumber numberWithFloat:3.0f];
    10          animation.autoreverses = YES;
     -          animation.duration = 10.0f;
     -      }
     -      return animation;
     -  }
```

Notice on line 4 that we are using a key path to initialize the animation. That key path is what the animation will change when it is applied. So, with any composition, we can change any of the exposed input keys via the same mechanism. This animation is added to the layer when a mouseDown event happens. If the animation is there, it is removed, and if it's not there, it's added. When it is added, the layer will change speed from 0.25 of its normal speed to 3 times its normal speed gradually.

I have only begun to scratch the surface of what is possible with Quartz Composer. It is a great tool and capable of making some really stunning animations. You owe it to your users to check it out and see whether there is something in your app that could benefit from a composition.

11.3 OpenGL Layers

From massively multiplayer online games to first-person shooters to medical imaging technology, OpenGL plays a major role in a lot of what we do with computers today. The support that is built into Core Animation for OpenGL allows us to combine the OpenGL code we already have with Core Animation layers so that we can integrate our OpenGL drawing with Core Animation.

In this section, I will walk you through a simple example that draws an OpenGL cube that rotates around a 3D axis. As you click, the rotating cube moves to where you clicked. Figure 11.5, on the following page is a screen shot with the application in action. The toggle button turns the rotation off and on.

To get OpenGL content into your layers, you simply subclass CAOpen-GLLayer and override a couple of methods. Here is the override of the init method:

MediaLayers/OpenGLLayer/OpenGLLayer.m

```
- (id)init {
  self = [super init];
  self.animate = YES;
  self.asynchronous = YES;
  return self;
}
```

Here we are setting the animated and asynchronous properties to YES. The asynchronous property specifies whether the layer is continuously updated.

When asynchronous is YES, the layer will periodically receive a canDraw-InCGLContext:pixelFormat:forLayerTime:displayTime: method call. If YES is returned, then drawInCGLContext:pixelFormat:forLayerTime:displayTime: is

Figure 11.5: QUARTZ COMPOSER LAYER IN ACTION

called. If NO is returned, then the draw... method is not called. So if your OpenGL content animates, then you want to set asynchronous to YES. This custom layer selectively animates depending on whether the animate flag is YES or NO. The canDraw... method is overridden so that the draw... method is called only if animate is YES. Here is the code:

MediaLayers/OpenGLLayer/OpenGLLayer.m

```
- (BOOL)canDrawInCGLContext:(CGLContextObj)glContext
              pixelFormat:(CGLPixelFormatObj)pixelFormat
             forLayerTime:(CFTimeInterval)timeInterval
             displayTime:(const CVTimeStamp *)timeStamp {
  if(NO == self.animate) {
    previousTime = 0.0;
  }
  return self.animate;
}
```

In this method, we reset the previousTime property to zero because we use that in our calculations in the draw... method.

Let's look at that code next:

MediaLayers/OpenGLLayer/OpenGLLayer.m

```
Line 1  - (void)drawInCGLContext:(CGLContextObj)glContext
     -                 pixelFormat:(CGLPixelFormatObj)pixelFormat
     -                forLayerTime:(CFTimeInterval)interval
     -                 displayTime:(const CVTimeStamp *)timeStamp {
     5    glClearColor(0.0f, 0.0f, 0.0f, 0.0f);
     -    glClear(GL_COLOR_BUFFER_BIT | GL_DEPTH_BUFFER_BIT);
     -    glEnable(GL_DEPTH_TEST);
     -    glHint(GL_LINE_SMOOTH_HINT, GL_NICEST);
     -    glHint(GL_POLYGON_SMOOTH_HINT, GL_NICEST);
    10    if(previousTime == 0) {
     -      previousTime = interval;
     -    }
     -    rotation += 15.0 * (interval - previousTime);
     -    glLoadIdentity();
    15    GLdouble comp = 1.0f/sqrt(3.0f);
     -    glRotatef(rotation, comp, comp, comp);
     -    [self drawCube];
     -    glFlush();
     -    previousTime = interval;
    20    glDisable(GL_DEPTH_TEST);
     -    glHint(GL_LINE_SMOOTH_HINT, GL_DONT_CARE);
     -    glHint(GL_POLYGON_SMOOTH_HINT, GL_DONT_CARE);
     -  }
```

Most of this is OpenGL code, and I won't spend any time on it. However, on line 17, the drawCube is called, which is responsible for pushing the vertices and such into the OpenGL pipeline.

One other aspect to keep in mind when dealing with OpenGL layers is that the default pixel format that it builds makes a bunch of assumptions you might not like. To get the layer to use the pixel format you do like, you override the copyCGLPixelFormatForDisplayMask: method and return whatever pixel format you want. In particular, when drawing 3D scenes (as opposed to just textures), you might want to have a depth buffer (which is off by default). Here is the code for this example:

MediaLayers/OpenGLLayer/OpenGLLayer.m

```
- (CGLPixelFormatObj)copyCGLPixelFormatForDisplayMask:(uint32_t)mask {
  CGLPixelFormatAttribute attribs[] =
  {
    kCGLPFAAccelerated,
    kCGLPFADoubleBuffer,
    kCGLPFAColorSize, 24,
    kCGLPFADepthSize, 16,
    0
  };
```

```
CGLPixelFormatObj pixelFormatObj = NULL;
GLint numPixelFormats = 0;

CGLChoosePixelFormat(attribs, &pixelFormatObj, &numPixelFormats);
return pixelFormatObj;
}
```

In this chapter, we covered three additional layer types that we didn't look at previously, and you have learned how to integrate QuickTime, Quartz Composer compositions, and OpenGL content into your applications. I hope that your head is buzzing with all the really cool and amazing possibilities this kind of integration technology opens up for you to use in your apps.

It is only by following your deepest instinct that you can lead a rich life, and if you let your fear of consequence prevent you from following your deepest instinct, then your life will be safe, expedient, and thin.

▶ Katharine Butler Hathaway

Chapter 12

Core Animation on the iPhone

Despite that our first look at Core Animation was in the Mac OS X Leopard release, at the launch of the iPhone SDK Apple explained that Core Animation was written for the iPhone. The intuitive and beautiful UI that makes the iPhone the great piece of technology that it is owes its existence to the animation capabilities that are built into Core Animation. Of course, there is a lot more to the iPhone and its SDK than Core Animation, but the underlying nature of the UI is all Core Animation.

One of the best aspects of Core Animation on the iPhone is its similarity with Core Animation on Mac OS X. We have many of the classes we have come to know; CABasicAnimation is there as well as CAMediaTiming and most others. Of course, there are a few differences because of the iPhone's unique nature. The differences between Core Animation on Mac OS X and the iPhone OS are the topic of this chapter.

12.1 Cocoa Touch

Cocoa Touch is the iPhone equivalent of Cocoa from Mac OS X. Many of the concepts we have come to know in Cocoa are present in Cocoa Touch. AppKit on Mac OS X has NSResponder to respond to events of all types from a Mac application. The iPhone has UIResponder to carry out the same functionality. In fact, most of the conceptual space that you have mastered in building Cocoa applications for the Mac will apply directly to the Cocoa Touch frameworks on the iPhone.

As with AppKit, Core Animation is tightly integrated with UIKit on the iPhone. Actually, the integration is even tighter on the iPhone OS. In AppKit, when you want to use layers, you have to explicitly make a view layer-backed. All views (instances and subclasses of UIView) on the iPhone are backed by a CALayer from creation to destruction.

The tight integration with UIView actually makes it more likely that you won't need to use Core Animation directly to build your dynamic user interface. UIView is actually a thin cover over a CALayer; you can think of the view as a CALayer with some convenience methods to handle events. Let's take a look at an example to see just how easy it is to add animation to your Cocoa Touch–based user interface. In Figure 12.1, on the next page, you can see the sample application. The simple box at the bottom moves to wherever you tap with a nice smooth animation.

So, let's take a look at the code that will make this simple animation work. Here is the code for the touchesEnded:withEvent: method:

CAOniPhone/Simple/Classes/MyView.m

```
Line 1   - (void)touchesEnded:(NSSet *)touches withEvent:(UIEvent *)event {
     -       UITouch *touch = touches.anyObject;
     -       [UIView beginAnimations:@"center" context:nil];
     -       self.boxView.center = [touch locationInView:self];
     5       [UIView commitAnimations];
     -   }
```

On line 3, the beginAnimation:context: is called. This method starts what is called an *animation block*. All the animations that are triggered within a block start and end at the same time. So, for example, you could have a fade animation in addition to this position change animation happening at the same time as long as they were both in the same animation block. On line 4, the value for the center of the view is changed. This change is animated since it happened in an animation block. An animation block is any set of property changes that are made between the beginAnimation:context: and commitAnimations method calls. This is similar to getting the animator proxy that we saw in animating AppKit views. On line 5, the call to commitAnimations causes the animations to start.

Custom Animations

Just as with AppKit, we can provide our own animations in UIKit to override the defaults and get more control over the animation. Unlike an NSView, every UIView has a layer. The UIView becomes the layer's delegate, so in order to set up our own animations, we simply override the delegate method animationForLayer:forKey: and return the animation we want for the key we are interested in customizing.

Figure 12.1: SIMPLE UIKIT INTERFACE

Here is the code that provides a custom animation for the position change:

CAOniPhone/Simple/Classes/BoxView.m

```
- (id<CAAction>)actionForLayer:(CALayer *)layer forKey:(NSString *)key {
  id<CAAction> animation = nil;
  if([key isEqualToString:@"position"]) {
    animation = [CABasicAnimation animation];
    ((CABasicAnimation*)animation).duration = 1.0f;
  } else {
    animation = [super actionForLayer:layer forKey:key];
  }
  return animation;
}
```

As you will undoubtedly notice, this code looks a lot like the delegate methods we wrote to customize the animation of our layers on Mac OS X. The similarity is pervasive throughout Core Animation on the iPhone. We will get to some of the differences shortly, but it's remarkably the same writing Core Animation code for the iPhone, and for Mac OS X.

Most of what is possible with Core Animation and AppKit is possible with UIKit. The one exception is the lack of Core Image on the iPhone. Without Core Image, it is not possible for us to specify custom transitions or filters for our UIViews.

12.2 Layers and Animations

Most of the layers that you have come to know are the same on the iPhone. The root of the layer class hierarchy is CALayer as expected. The only differences for this class are the removal of the filter-related attributes; since Core Image is not available, these properties don't make sense. The other things you have come to know, however, are there. Layers still implicitly animate any property change, and you can still put an image into a layer with the contents property.

The CATiledLayer and CAScrollLayer classes are also substantially the same as they are on Mac OS X. The tiled layer is used for smaller images given the smaller memory space available on the iPhone compared to a Mac. Whereas a typical Leopard-era Mac can easily display an image with 2048 by 2048 pixels, the iPhone does about 1/4th the pixels at 1024 by 1024.

The iPhone does not include Quartz Composer or any of its frameworks, so rendering a Quartz Composer composition on the iPhone is not currently possible. Since we can't display a composition, the layer to render them is absent from the iPhone.

In a similar manner, QuickTime is not present on the iPhone (well, parts of it are, but it's not accessible except through the Media Player framework). So, we don't have the QuickTime layer support either. This ends up not being much of a restriction. We can play movies on the iPhone with the Media Player framework. Besides, the types of interactions and interfaces we might build with the QuickTime layer functionality don't make as much sense on the iPhone.

OpenGL is available on the iPhone in the form of OpenGL ES. OpenGL ES is a trimmed-down API set for OpenGL with basically all the functionality without all the extra means to specify things that exist in OpenGL proper. Consider polygons: in OpenGL, you can pass triangles or quads; when you pass a quad, though, the driver just converts it to triangles. OpenGL ES requires us to pass data in as triangles instead of of allowing quads. This not only makes the driver much simpler, but it also makes it more efficient. There are several other trade-offs like this, but for the most part OpenGL ES is OpenGL. For details on the differences, visit the Khronos website at http://www.khronos.org/opengles/.

Let's dive into an example of using Core Animation on the iPhone. In this example, you will load a photo from the photo library on your iPod Touch or iPhone, display it in a layer, and then divide the layer into many smaller layers and send them flying off the screen. In Figure 12.2, on the following page, you can see a photo selected and displayed.

The code uses the typical approach of creating a UIImagePickerController with a source type of UIImagePickerControllerSourceTypePhotoLibrary. After the user chooses which photo to use, the delegate method imagePickerController:didFinishPickingImage:editingInfo: is called. Let's look at the code for that method:

CAOniPhone/Confetti/Classes/RootController.m

```
Line 1  - (void)imagePickerController:(UIImagePickerController *)picker
                 didFinishPickingImage:(UIImage *)newImage
                          editingInfo:(NSDictionary *)editingInfo {
           self.image = newImage;
    5      drawnImage = [self scaleAndCropImage:self.image];
           imageLayer.contents = (id)drawnImage;
           [[picker parentViewController] dismissModalViewControllerAnimated:YES];
        }
```

Figure 12.2: Image displayed in layer

First this method copies a reference to the selected image on line 4. Then the image is scaled and cropped so that it fits into the layer properly via a call to scaleAndCropImage:. The image is then placed into the contents of the image layer, and the image picker controller is dismissed. Except for the image picker controller, this process is no different from what you'd do if this were a Mac program.

In Figure 12.3, on the next page, you can see the image after being broken into several pieces and sent flying off the screen. Next up, we will look at the code that makes the image pieces and sends them flying.

The pop: method does two things; first it divides up the image into multiple pieces, creating a new layer for each piece of the image, and then each of the smaller layers is added to the image layer as sublayers. Here is the code:

CAOniPhone/Confetti/Classes/RootController.m

```
Line 1   - (void)pop:(id)sender {
           if(nil != imageLayer.contents) {
             CGSize imageSize = CGSizeMake(CGImageGetWidth(drawnImage),
                                           CGImageGetHeight(drawnImage));
      5      NSMutableArray *layers = [NSMutableArray array];
             for(int x = 0;x < kXSlices;x++) {
               for(int y = 0;y < kYSlices;y++) {
                 CGRect frame = CGRectMake((imageSize.width / kXSlices) * x,
                                           (imageSize.height / kYSlices) * y,
     10                                     imageSize.width / kXSlices,
                                           imageSize.height / kYSlices);
                 CALayer *layer = [CALayer layer];
                 layer.frame = frame;
                 layer.actions = [NSDictionary dictionaryWithObject:
     15                            [self animationForX:x Y:y imageSize:imageSize]
                                                         forKey:@"opacity"];
                 CGImageRef subimage = CGImageCreateWithImageInRect(drawnImage, frame);
                 layer.contents = (id)subimage;
                 CFRelease(subimage);
     20          [layers addObject:layer];
               }
             }
             for(CALayer *layer in layers) {
               [imageLayer addSublayer:layer];
     25        layer.opacity = 0.0f;
             }
             imageLayer.contents = nil;
           }
         }
```

This code is fairly straightforward Quartz code that you can learn more about in the Quartz book ([GL06]). Notice on line 16 that the actions

Figure 12.3: Image flying off the screen

dictionary is being used to add a custom animation to the layer. Then, on line 25, the animation is being triggered by changing the opacity.

The animation is a group containing two animations. The first is the opacity animation that fades out the pieces as they move farther and farther away from their starting points. The second is a position animation that moves the pieces from their start point to a random point off the screen in the same quadrant that the piece started in (top right, bottom left, and so on). The code to create the animations is here:

CAOniPhone/Confetti/Classes/RootController.m

```
Line 1   - (CAAnimation *)animationForX:(NSInteger)x Y:(NSInteger)y
                           imageSize:(CGSize)size {
             // return a group animation, one for opacity from 1 to zero and a keyframe
             // with a path appropriate for the x and y coords
      5      CAAnimationGroup *group = [CAAnimationGroup animation];
             group.delegate = self;
             group.duration = 2.0f;

             CABasicAnimation *opacity = [CABasicAnimation
     10                                  animationWithKeyPath:@"opacity"];
             opacity.fromValue = [NSNumber numberWithDouble:1.0f];
             opacity.toValue = [NSNumber numberWithDouble:0.0f];

             CABasicAnimation *position = [CABasicAnimation
     15                                  animationWithKeyPath:@"position"];
             position.timingFunction = [CAMediaTimingFunction
                                  functionWithName:kCAMediaTimingFunctionEaseIn];
             CGPoint dest = [self randomDestinationX:x Y:y imageSize:size];
             position.toValue = [NSValue valueWithCGPoint:dest];
     20
             group.animations = [NSArray arrayWithObjects:opacity, position, nil];
             return group;
         }
```

The code for creating the group animation is similar to what we saw before when creating group animations. The two contained animations are created on lines 10 and 14 and then added to the group on line 21.

As you can see, most of what you have learned about Core Animation applies directly to writing applications with the iPhone SDK. It is important, though, to keep in mind the way applications work on the iPhone. Simply copying code from a working Mac application over to run on the iPhone might mean the app compiles and runs, but the user experience will be less than ideal. Instead, trim the application down to the things people will want to use when on the go.

12.3 OpenGL Layers

OpenGL on the iPhone is done only via a Core Animation layer. This is different from on the Mac in that Core Animation is just one of many options in getting OpenGL content to the screen. In this section, you will learn how to get a layer to do your OpenGL drawing on.

To get a Core Animation layer to do your OpenGL drawing on, you must subclass UIView and override the layerClass method to return the CAEAGLLayer class. The layerClass method returns CALayer by default and is called when setting up the view. This method gives us the chance to customize what type of backing store is used for our views (recall that on the iPhone all views are backed by layers).

Now that the view is set up to use OpenGL, the context needs to be initialized. Currently there are two parts to that: first the drawableProperties property is initialized on the layer, and then a frame buffer is constructed. Once the surface is configured and the frame buffer is created and configured, the application is ready to accept OpenGL drawing commands. As with all things OpenGL, the options are many, and explaining them in any detail is beyond the scope of this book (take a look at the Blue Book [WLH07] for a great "getting started with OpenGL" book). Luckily, all this configuration and creation is done for us via the OpenGL ES application template that is part of Xcode.

Let's take a quick look at the code provided by the template, starting with the code to configure the layer:

```
CAOniPhone/RotatingBox/Classes/EAGLView.m
```
```
CAEAGLLayer *eaglLayer = (CAEAGLLayer *)self.layer;
eaglLayer.opaque = YES;
eaglLayer.drawableProperties = [NSDictionary dictionaryWithObjectsAndKeys:
                [NSNumber numberWithBool:FALSE],
                kEAGLDrawablePropertyRetainedBacking,
                kEAGLColorFormatRGBA8,
                kEAGLDrawablePropertyColorFormat, nil];
```

This configuration does not provide retained backing and specifies the RGBA 8 color format (via the kEAGLColorFormatRGBA8 constant). There are many, many options for what kind of color format to use. Given the more limited memory bandwidth available on the iPhone, it is important to use the smallest types (including color formats) that work for your application.

Next, the EAGLContext is configured:

CAOniPhone/RotatingBox/Classes/EAGLView.m

```
Line 1  context = [[EAGLContext alloc] initWithAPI:kEAGLRenderingAPIOpenGLES1];
    -   if (!context || ![EAGLContext setCurrentContext:context]) {
    -           [self release];
    -           return nil;
    5   }
```

Specifying the API level on line 1 allows us to specify which version of the API we'd like to use. For iPhone OS 2.0, the value must be kEAGLRenderingAPIOpenGLES1, but expect the list to expand to future releases of the iPhone OS. Next we set the current context.

In layoutSubviews, set the current context and recreate the frame buffer. (For the gnarly Open GL stuff, you will have to consult the blue book: [WLH07].) And if all goes well the application is ready to draw its first frame. Here is the code:

CAOniPhone/RotatingBox/Classes/EAGLView.m

```
- (void)layoutSubviews {
        [EAGLContext setCurrentContext:context];
        [self destroyFramebuffer];
        [self createFramebuffer];
        [self drawView];
}
```

Finally let's look at the drawing code:

CAOniPhone/RotatingBox/Classes/EAGLView.m

```
Line 1  - (void)drawView {
    -           const GLfloat squareVertices[] = {
    -                   -0.5f, -0.5f,
    -                   0.5f,  -0.5f,
    5                   -0.5f,  0.5f,
    -                   0.5f,   0.5f,
    -           };
    -           const GLubyte squareColors[] = {
    -                   255, 255,   0, 255,
    10                  0,   255, 255, 255,
    -                   0,    0,   0,   0,
    -                   255,   0, 255, 255,
    -           };
    -
    15          [EAGLContext setCurrentContext:context];
    -
    -           glBindFramebufferOES(GL_FRAMEBUFFER_OES, viewFramebuffer);
    -           glViewport(0, 0, backingWidth, backingHeight);
    -
```

```
20        glMatrixMode(GL_PROJECTION);
 -        glLoadIdentity();
 -        glOrthof(-1.0f, 1.0f, -1.5f, 1.5f, -1.0f, 1.0f);
 -        glMatrixMode(GL_MODELVIEW);
 -        glRotatef(3.0f, 0.0f, 0.0f, 1.0f);
25
 -        glClearColor(0.5f, 0.5f, 0.5f, 1.0f);
 -        glClear(GL_COLOR_BUFFER_BIT);
 -
 -        glVertexPointer(2, GL_FLOAT, 0, squareVertices);
30        glEnableClientState(GL_VERTEX_ARRAY);
 -        glColorPointer(4, GL_UNSIGNED_BYTE, 0, squareColors);
 -        glEnableClientState(GL_COLOR_ARRAY);
 -
 -        glDrawArrays(GL_TRIANGLE_STRIP, 0, 4);
35
 -        glBindRenderbufferOES(GL_RENDERBUFFER_OES, viewRenderbuffer);
 -        [context presentRenderbuffer:GL_RENDERBUFFER_OES];
 -    }
```

On line 15, the current context is set to the context that was previously
created. It is important to always set the context before you draw, or
unpredictable results can occur. Next, the vertex data is pushed on line
29. Now that OpenGL has the data, all that remains is to draw it via
the call to glDrawArrays() on line 34. In Figure 12.4, on the facing page,
you can see what this code looks like when it's running.

In this chapter, we covered the differences between Core Animation on
the iPhone and Core Animation on Mac OS X. With the knowledge you
have gained, you can now write stunning applications for both platforms. I can't wait to see what you come up with.

Figure 12.4: ROTATING BOX

Bibliography

[App06]   Apple, Inc.   Cocoa Drawing Tips.   http://developer.
            apple.com/documentation/Performance/Conceptual/
            Drawing/Articles/CocoaDrawingTips.html#//apple_ref/doc/uid/
            TP40001470-BAJJAFGE, 2006.

[App07a]   Apple, Inc. Introduction to Quartz 2D Programming Guide.
            http://developer.apple.com/documentation/GraphicsImaging/
            Conceptual/drawingwithquartz2d/dq_intro/chapter_1_section_1.
            html, 2007.

[App07b]   Apple, Inc. Introduction to Quartz Composer User Guide.
            http://developer.apple.com/documentation/GraphicsImaging/
            Conceptual/QuartzComposerUserGuide/qc_intro/chapter_1_
            section_1.html, 2007.

[App08a]   Apple, Inc. Introduction to Core Animation Programming
            Guide.   http://developer.apple.com/documentation/Cocoa/
            Conceptual/CoreAnimation_guide/Introduction/Introduction.html,
            2008.

[App08b]   Apple, Inc. Introduction to Core Image Programming Guide.
            http://developer.apple.com/documentation/GraphicsImaging/
            Conceptual/CoreImaging/ci_intro/chapter_1_section_1.html,
            2008.

[App08c]   Apple, Inc.   Opengl Programming Guide for Mac OS X.
            http://developer.apple.com/documentation/GraphicsImaging/
            Conceptual/OpenGL-MacProgGuide/opengl_intro/chapter_1_
            section_1.html, 2008.

[GL06]   David Gelphman and Bunny Laden. *Programming with
            Quartz, 2D and PDF Graphics in Mac OS X.* Morgan Kauf-
            man, San Francisco, 2006.

[WLH07]   Richard S. Wright, Jr., Benjamin Lipchak, and Nicholas Haemel. *OpenGL SuperBible*. Addison Wesley Longman, Reading, MA, fourth edition, 2007.

Index

More Mac titles

Learn tips and tricks for our favorite Mac text editor, and dig into a Pragmatic treasure trove for the iPhone.

TextMate

If you're coding Ruby or Rails on a Mac, then you owe it to yourself to get the TextMate editor. And, once you're using TextMate, you owe it to yourself to pick up this book. It's packed with information that will help you automate all your editing tasks, saving you time to concentrate on the important stuff. Use snippets to insert boilerplate code and refactorings to move stuff around. Learn how to write your own extensions to customize it to the way you work.

TextMate: Power Editing for the Mac
James Edward Gray II
(200 pages) ISBN: 0-9787392-3-X. $29.95
http://pragprog.com/titles/textmate

iPhone SDK Development

Jump into application development for today's most remarkable mobile communications platform, the Pragmatic way. This Pragmatic guide takes you through the tools and APIs, the same ones Apple uses for its applications, that you can use to create your own software for the iPhone and iPod touch. Packed with useful examples, this book will give you both the big-picture concepts and the everyday "gotcha" details that developers need to make the most of the beauty and power of the iPhone OS platform.

iPhone SDK Development
Bill Dudney, Chris Adamson, Marcel Molina
(200 pages) ISBN: 978-1-9343562-5-8. $38.95
http://pragprog.com/titles/amiphd

Web 2.0

Welcome to the Web, version 2.0. You need some help to tame the wild technologies out there.

Prototype and script.aculo.us

Tired of getting swamped in the nitty-gritty of cross-browser, Web 2.0–grade JavaScript? Get back in the game with Prototype and script.aculo.us, two extremely popular JavaScript libraries that make it a walk in the park. Be it Ajax, drag and drop, autocompletion, advanced visual effects, or many other great features, all you need is write one or two lines of script that look so good they could almost pass for Ruby code!

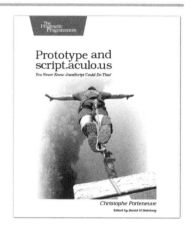

Prototype and script.aculo.us: You never knew JavaScript could do this!
Christophe Porteneuve
(330 pages) ISBN: 1-934356-01-8. $34.95
http://pragprog.com/titles/cppsu

Design Accessible Web Sites

The 2000 U.S. Census revealed that 12% of the population is severely disabled. Sometime in the next two decades, one in five Americans will be older than 65. Section 508 of the Americans with Disabilities Act requires your website to provide *equivalent access* to all potential users. But beyond the law, it is both good manners and good business to make your site accessible to everyone. This book shows you how to design sites that excel for all audiences.

Design Accessible Web Sites: 36 Keys to Creating Content for All Audiences and Platforms
Jeremy Sydik
(304 pages) ISBN: 978-1-9343560-2-9. $34.95
http://pragprog.com/titles/jsaccess

Getting It Done

Start with the habits of an agile developer and use the team practices of successful agile teams, and your project will fly over the finish line.

Practices of an Agile Developer

Agility is all about using feedback to respond to change. Learn how to • apply the principles of agility throughout the software development process • establish and maintain an agile working environment • deliver what users really want • use personal agile techniques for better coding and debugging • use effective collaborative techniques for better teamwork • move to an agile approach

Practices of an Agile Developer:
Working in the Real World
Venkat Subramaniam and Andy Hunt
(189 pages) ISBN: 0-9745140-8-X. $29.95
http://pragprog.com/titles/pad

Ship It!

Page after page of solid advice, all tried and tested in the real world. This book offers a collection of tips that show you what tools a successful team has to use, and how to use them well. You'll get quick, easy-to-follow advice on modern techniques and when they should be applied. **You need this book if:** • You're frustrated at lack of progress on your project. • You want to make yourself and your team more valuable. • You've looked at methodologies such as Extreme Programming (XP) and felt they were too, well, extreme. • You've looked at the Rational Unified Process (RUP) or CMM/I methods and cringed at the learning curve and costs. • **You need to get software out the door without excuses**

Ship It! A Practical Guide to Successful Software
Projects
Jared Richardson and Will Gwaltney
(200 pages) ISBN: 0-9745140-4-7. $29.95
http://pragprog.com/titles/prj

Agile Practices

From revving up your brain to mining your team, we've got the stuff you need to know.

Pragmatic Thinking and Learning

Software development happens in your head. Not in an editor, IDE, or design tool. In this book by Pragmatic Programmer Andy Hunt, you'll learn how our brains are wired, and how to take advantage of your brain's architecture. You'll master new tricks and tips to learn more, faster, and retain more of what you learn.

• Use the Dreyfus Model of Skill Acquisition to become more expert • Leverage the architecture of the brain to strengthen different thinking modes
• Avoid common "known bugs" in your mind
• Learn more deliberately and more effectively
• Manage knowledge more efficiently

Pragmatic Thinking and Learning:
Refactor your Wetware
Andy Hunt
(288 pages) ISBN: 978-1-9343560-5-0. $34.95
http://pragprog.com/titles/ahptl

Agile Retrospectives

Mine the experience of your software development team continually throughout the life of the project. Rather than waiting until the end of the project—as with a traditional retrospective, when it's too late to help—agile retrospectives help you adjust to change *today*.

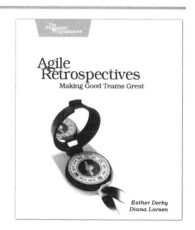

The tools and recipes in this book will help you uncover and solve hidden (and not-so-hidden) problems with your technology, your methodology, and those difficult "people issues" on your team.

Agile Retrospectives: Making Good Teams Great
Esther Derby and Diana Larsen
(170 pages) ISBN: 0-9776166-4-9. $29.95
http://pragprog.com/titles/dlret

Ruby Starts Here

If you're programming in Ruby, you need the new PickAxe Book and the new Rails book.

Programming Ruby 1.9 (The Pickaxe for 1.9)

The Pickaxe book, named for the tool on the cover, is the definitive reference to this highly-regarded language.

• Up-to-date and expanded for Ruby version 1.9
• Complete documentation of all the built-in classes, modules, and methods • Complete descriptions of all standard libraries • Learn more about Ruby's web tools, unit testing, and programming philosophy

Programming Ruby 1.9: The Pragmatic Programmer's Guide for Ruby 1.9
Dave Thomas with Chad Fowler and Andy Hunt
(900 pages) ISBN: 978-1-9343560-8-1. $49.95
http://pragprog.com/titles/ruby3

Agile Web Development with Rails

Rails is a full-stack, open-source web framework, with integrated support for unit, functional, and integration testing. It enforces good design principles, consistency of code across your team (and across your organization), and proper release management. This is the newly updated Third Edition, which goes beyond the award winning previous editions with new material covering the latest advances in Rails 2.0.

Agile Web Development with Rails: Third Edition
Sam Ruby, Dave Thomas, and David Heinemeier Hansson, et al.
(750 pages) ISBN: 978-1-9343561-6-6. $43.95
http://pragprog.com/titles/rails3

Get Groovy

Expand your horizons with Groovy, and tame the wild Java VM.

Programming Groovy

Programming Groovy will help you learn the necessary fundamentals of programming in Groovy. You'll see how to use Groovy to do advanced programming techniques, including meta programming, builders, unit testing with mock objects, processing XML, working with databases and creating your own domain-specific languages (DSLs).

Programming Groovy Dynamic Productivity for the Java Developer
Venkat Subramaniam
(320 pages) ISBN: 978-1-9343560-9-8. $34.95
http://pragprog.com/titles/vslg

Groovy Recipes

See how to speed up nearly every aspect of the development process using *Groovy Recipes*. Groovy makes mundane file management tasks like copying and renaming files trivial. Reading and writing XML has never been easier with XmlParsers and XmlBuilders. Breathe new life into arrays, maps, and lists with a number of convenience methods. Learn all about Grails, and go beyond HTML into the world of Web Services: REST, JSON, Atom, Podcasting, and much much more.

Groovy Recipes: Greasing the Wheels of Java
Scott Davis
(264 pages) ISBN: 978-0-9787392-9-4. $34.95
http://pragprog.com/titles/sdgrvr

Explore New Worlds

Tips for wrangling Ubuntu Linux, and a reliable approach to massively parallel programming.

Ubuntu Kung Fu

Award-winning Linux author Keir Thomas gets down and dirty with Ubuntu to provide over 300 concise tips that enhance productivity, avoid annoyances, and simply get the most from Ubuntu. You'll find many unique tips here that can't be found anywhere else.

You'll also get a crash course in Ubuntu's flavor of system administration. Whether you're new to Linux or an old hand, you'll find tips to make your day easier.

This is the Linux book for the rest of us.

Ubuntu Kung Fu: Tips, Tricks, Hints, and Hacks
Keir Thomas
(400 pages) ISBN: 978-1-9343562-2-7. $34.95
http://pragprog.com/titles/ktuk

Programming Erlang

Learn how to write truly concurrent programs— programs that run on dozens or even hundreds of local and remote processors. See how to write high-reliability applications—even in the face of network and hardware failure—using the Erlang programming language.

Programming Erlang: Software for a Concurrent World
Joe Armstrong
(536 pages) ISBN: 1-934356-00-X. $36.95
http://pragprog.com/titles/jaerlang

The Pragmatic Bookshelf

The Pragmatic Bookshelf features books written by developers for developers. The titles continue the well-known Pragmatic Programmer style and continue to garner awards and rave reviews. As development gets more and more difficult, the Pragmatic Programmers will be there with more titles and products to help you stay on top of your game.

Visit Us Online

Core Animation for Mac OS X and the iPhone's Home Page
http://pragprog.com/titles/bdcora
Source code from this book, errata, and other resources. Come give us feedback, too!

Register for Updates
http://pragprog.com/updates
Be notified when updates and new books become available.

Join the Community
http://pragprog.com/community
Read our weblogs, join our online discussions, participate in our mailing list, interact with our wiki, and benefit from the experience of other Pragmatic Programmers.

New and Noteworthy
http://pragprog.com/news
Check out the latest pragmatic developments in the news.

Save on the PDF

Save on the PDF version of this book. Owning the paper version of this book entitles you to purchase the PDF version at a terrific discount. The PDF is great for carrying around on your laptop. It's hyperlinked, has color, and is fully searchable.

Buy it now at pragprog.com/coupon.

Contact Us

Phone Orders:	1-800-699-PROG (+1 919 847 3884)
Online Orders:	www.pragprog.com/catalog
Customer Service:	orders@pragprog.com
Non-English Versions:	translations@pragprog.com
Pragmatic Teaching:	academic@pragprog.com
Author Proposals:	proposals@pragprog.com